Autism Posit

A Practical Guide on Early Signs of Autism Every Parent Should Know and Positive Strategies to Help Your Child Develop Better.

Sharon Daven

© Copyright _____ 2021 - All rights reserved.

The content contained within this book may not be reproduced, duplicated or transmitted without direct written permission from the author or the publisher.

Under no circumstances will any blame or legal responsibility be held against the publisher, or author, for any damages, reparation, or monetary loss due to the information contained within this book. Either directly or indirectly. You are responsible for your own choices, actions, and results.

<u>Legal Notice:</u>

This book is copyright protected. This book is only for personal use. You cannot amend, distribute, sell, use, quote or paraphrase any part, or the content within this book, without the consent of the author or publisher.

Disclaimer Notice:

Please note the information contained within this document is for educational and entertainment purposes only. All effort has been executed to present accurate, up to date, and reliable, complete information. No warranties of any kind are declared or implied. Readers acknowledge that the author is not engaging in the rendering of legal, financial, medical or professional advice. The content within this book has been derived from various sources. Please consult a licensed professional before attempting any techniques outlined in this book.

By reading this document, the reader agrees that under no circumstances is the author responsible for any losses, direct or indirect, which are incurred as a result of the use of the information contained within this document, including, but not limited to, — errors, omissions, or inaccuracies.

Your Free Gift

As a way of saying thanks for your purchase, I'm offering this book ***BABY SAFETY TIPS*** for **FREE** to my readers.

To get instant access **SCAN THE QR CODE:**

Inside this book, you will discover:

- 12-Must have products that will keep your child safe around the home

- Traveling with a baby checklist.

- How to reduce the risk of poisoning in your house hold.

- Toy Safety Tips.

- Safe bedding practices for infants

If you want to know how to keep your baby safe, make sure to grab this **FREE** book now.

Table of Content

INTRODUCTION 13

CHAPTER ONE 19

UNDERSTANDING AUTISM 19

CAUSES OF AUTISM 24

KINDS OF AUTISM 32

CHAPTER TWO 39

EARLY SIGNS OF AUTISM 39

Difficulty with communication and interaction 41

CHAPTER THREE 64

ACCEPTING YOUR AUTISTIC CHILD 64

MISCONCEPTIONS OF AUTISM 71

POST DIAGNOSIS EXPERIENCE 85

7 Things You Should Research About in Post Diagnosis 92

CHAPTER FOUR 96

POSITIVE REINFORCEMENT 96

WHY DO PEOPLE DETEST THIS STRATEGY? 98

WHY YOU SHOULD USE POSITIVE REINFORCEMENT 102

HOW TO USE POSITIVE REINFORCEMENT 105

COMMON POSITIVE REINFORCEMENT MISTAKES MADE AND HOW TO CORRECT THEM 110

POSITIVE REINFORCEMENT: How to teach your child how to brush her teeth 114

CHAPTER FIVE 117

EXTINCTION 117

Where is Extinction needed? 118

Merits of Extinction Method 121

Demerits Of Extinction Method 123

Practical steps to using Extinction with your autistic child.. 125

HOW TO TEACH YOUR CHILD TOILET SKILLS WITH EXTINCTION. 128

10 practical steps to take to eliminate the problem behavior.. 130

How to Combine Positive Reinforcement and Extinction to Achieve behavioral change. 132

CHAPTER SIX.. 137

   DIFFERENTIAL REINFORCEMENT 137

HOW TO USE DIFFERENTIAL REINFORCEMENT 144

DIFFERENTIAL REINFORCEMENT: How to achieve a behavioral change in your child (Biting) 146

HOW TO STOP YOUR CHILD WITH AUTISM FROM BITING.. 148

CHAPTER SEVEN 151

   EMOTIONAL REGULATION 151

Benefits of emotions 154

Why emotional regulation is important?............. 156

How To Teach Your Autistic Child Emotional Regulation 157

    Understanding Emotions 162

Common Mistakes Parents Make During Their Child's Meltdown 163

    Managing Emotions.. 165

    How To Manage a Meltdown........................... 166

CHAPTER EIGHT 170

    SOCIAL SKILLS DEVELOPMENT.............. 170

Why you should teach your child social skills: .. 171

Examples of social skills...................................... 172

Milestones for Children's Development 175

How to Help an autistic child to develop social skills. 177

How to Measure Your Child's Social Skills 181

CHAPTER NINE 187

SENSORY REGULATION 187

Sensory Challenges 189

Sensory Regulation Strategies 191

CHAPTER TEN 196

EXPLORE THERAPY 196

Speech Therapy 197

Why Should I consider speech therapy for my autistic child? 198

Occupational therapy (OT) 204

Challenges Of Occupational Therapy 206

SOCIAL SKILLS TRAINING 208

Benefits of Social Skills Training for Autistic Children 211

    Challenges of Social Skill Training................. 213

Physical Therapy (PT) 215

    Physical Therapy Interventions 216

Cognitive-behavioral therapy (CBT) 218

Play therapy 221

Sensory Integration Therapy (SIT) 223

    Benefits of SIT... 226

        Some of the benefits of SIT include: 226

Music therapy and Art therapy 226

Benefits of Music therapy and art therapy for your child.. 228

CHAPTER ELEVEN... 230

LET'S HELP YOU FIND YOUR THERAPIST
.... 230

Autism Formal Diagnosis Process...................... 234

What Is the Cost of Autism Diagnosis?.............. 236

What Is the Scope of Your Health Insurance Coverage? 239

References 245

INTRODUCTION

Autism spectrum disorder (ASD) is a developmental condition that affects communication and behavior. People with ASD may struggle with social interaction, communication, and repetitive behaviors.

There is no one-size-fits-all approach to supporting autistic children, as each child's needs differ. However, there are several things that parents can do to help their children thrive.

This book is designed to give parents the information they need to support their autistic child. The book covers a wide range of topics, including:

- Understanding autism
- Identifying the early signs of autism
- Accepting your autistic child
- Using positive reinforcement to teach your child new skills

- Using extinction to manage challenging behaviors
- Helping your child regulate their emotions
- Developing your child's social skills
- Customizing your home for your child
- Choosing the suitable therapies
- Hiring a professional to help your child.

The book starts by providing an overview of autism, including the definition, causes, and types of autism. It also discusses the different ways that autism can manifest itself in children.

The objective of the first chapter is to equip you with the basic knowledge of autism, and give you straightforward answers to many questions that may have clouded your mind.

When I had my autistic child, I had numerous questions to which I was seeking answers. After fifteen years, I have written a book I wish was on the shelve for a woman like me.

Furthermore, we will explore the early signs of autism, which can be divided into three categories: communication, sensory needs, and behavioral signs (meltdowns).

It also provides information on how parents can identify their child as being on the autism spectrum. This is very important as many children with autism learn to live independently with the help of early intervention.

Early intervention refers to the educational and support system put in place to help little children who have slow development or disabilities to learn at their own pace to help them achieve highly independent lives.

Many autistic children have lived dependent because there was no early intervention. The second chapter seeks to end such occurrences as every parent who read this book will be able to identify the early signs of autism.

In addition, emphasis is made on the benefits of accepting your child for who they are, regardless of their autism. Many parents of autistic children live frustrated lives as they haven't accepted that their child may be born different but not abnormal.

I have worked with some parents who testified that accepting their child helped them take care of them and pay more attention to them. Also, the chapter also discussed ten common misconceptions about autism.

Beyond discussing autism, this book proffers help to parents on how to teach their autistic children life skills using a variety of method. The first method is the concept of positive reinforcement.

Positive reinforcement refers to rewarding a child for performing a desirable behavior or not completing an undesirable one. When parents are not enlightened about how to teach autistic children new skills, they get frustrated when they don't seem to be communicating with their children.

Furthermore, the extinction method is explained. This strategy is employed to help children to unlearn bad habits. Many parents reinforce bad habits without knowing it.

In this book, I showed you how to identify bad habits being reinforced and how to remove the reinforcement to stop the bad habit. We further explained the benefits of extinction and provided tips on implementing it effectively.

Children with autism have sensory needs, and we discussed sensory regulation for an autistic child at full length. This book provides tips on how to identify triggers for meltdowns and how to help your child calm down.

Also, we discussed how you can help your child develop social skills. This book provides information on the different types of social skills and how to teach them to your child.

Again, you will be exposed to how to customize your home to make it more comfortable and stimulating for your autistic child. This book also provides tips on identifying your child's sensory needs and creating a sensory-friendly environment.

I hope this book provides you with the necessary information to support your autistic child. Remember, you are not alone. Many resources are available to help you and your child on this journey.

CHAPTER ONE

UNDERSTANDING AUTISM

"Everyone is a genius. But if you judge a fish on its inability to climb a tree, it will live its whole life believing it is stupid." - Einstein.

Before anything else, you need to understand what autism is and why your child is referred to as a *special need*. At the end of this chapter, you will realize what exactly autism is, the causes of autism, and the variant manifestation of autism.

It is essential to know that understanding ASD empowers every parent to bond with their child and make sure they help them live independent lives. Ignorance has to be one of the worst problems we have in dealing with autism globally.

Surprisingly, the ignorance is not that people are unaware of autism; it is that they are clouded by multitudes of misconceptions. As a parent of an autistic child, seeking the correct information about autism is no longer optional.

Only the correct information can help you understand and support your child through his formative periods. Before I gave birth to Peter, my autistic child, I was not aware that anything of such existed.

Eventually, when I got exposed to autism, the misconceptions clouded me, just like many others. For some reason, the false and the half-truth stories get massive publicity, and that's why many organizations are investing massively in educating the public about autism.

The multiple Autism campaigns, both online and onsite, are geared towards sharing the correct information before the misconceptions destroy the lives of promising children and frustrated parents.

I really don't know what you have heard about autism. I don't believe I have the power to tell you to forget everything you must have heard or observed about this condition because we all will eventually have different experience.

Especially because all autistic children manifest autistic symptoms differently, but here is what I am asking from you today; pay close attention to everything I am about to tell you.

This chapter is not here to merely give you an autism introductory sermon. Instead, it is a functional instrument to help you understand why your children needs you to leverage some strategies to teach them life skills and help them live a productive life.

Although you will not write an autism exam in college, but your child will be the product of your knowledge; so, what will it be? Are you going to teach them new skills and help them unlearn the undesirable ones? If you will, then let's dive in.

Autism Spectrum Disorder is a neurodevelopmental disorder that affects how a person perceives, communicates, and interacts with the world around them.

Children with ASD are wired differently from the neuro typical children. I assume you already know everyone is unique, with or without autism. However, the children we refer to as autistic have common behavioral differences from the non-autistic children.

For example, most children with ASD have some communication difficulties such as inability to make eye contact, joint attention, etc.

These communication difficulties are what spurs parents to question why their children are different because these are basic behavioral expectations of a child. These questions hopefully lead to a diagnosis.

But in some case, an autistic child is not even noticed. It is either they are *masking*, or the environment is friendly. We say an autistic child is masking when they consciously or unconsciously hide the characteristics of the autistic identity.

The autistic identity is the signs of autism that will be discussed in the following chapter. As such, autistic children are wired differently, know that no two autistic children are the same.

CAUSES OF AUTISM

I can write a helpful handbook to help you navigate your parenting without mentioning the causes of autism because I do not see what use it will be to you.

However, when I was planning this book's content, I stepped into your shoes, and one of the bugging questions I heard in my ears was, "Why does she have autism? Where did it come from? Was I the cause? Could I have prevented it?"

I was haunted by that question years ago when my last son was diagnosed with autism. He was my last child, and I remember wishing I never got pregnant. My husband and I wanted to have three children, and five years after having my third child, I discovered I was pregnant.

So, I understand that curiosity that makes you surf the internet and devour every possible information. Most parents feel terrible when they confirm that their children are wired differently, especially when they have heard a thousand and one misconceptions about autism.

Here is one wonderful message I want you to get, even if you don't get anything else from this whole chapter; it is not your fault that your child has autism, and I honestly think there is nothing you would have done differently to prevent it from happening this way.

And it is no pep talk; I am telling you the truth. Leave the scientists to bother themselves about the causes and prevention of autism; if you have children, let's focus on them.

Humorously, the author of the book; "Your child is not broken," said the only way to prevent autism is that autistic individuals should stop having sex. I remember laughing at her solution, but it is true.

Stop thinking about how to prevent autism and start thinking about how to take care of your child. Autism is not a plague, a death sentence or the worst thing that can happen to you.

People with autism can live an independent life if they are diagnosed early and helped. Reading this book, regardless of many other things you must do, proves that you are willing and interested to be the best help you can possibly be to your child.

There are two major causes of autism, and they include genetic and environmental causes.

Genetic factors. Although the causes of autism have remained a mystery, research has revealed that some individuals are more susceptible to being born autistic than others genetically.

The above assertions are based on a published study. The study involved the examination of autistic people's close relatives. The areas the studied are as listed below:

- ✓ Studies on identical twins have shown that if one child is born autistic, the other child is affected 36-95% of the time, while in the case of a non-identical twin, there is 31% of the other being autistic if one has autism.

- ✓ Also, it has been determined that parents who have a child with autism have a 2-18 % chance of having another autistic child.

Following the stats stated, you see that one cause of autism is simply because of their genes. A gene is the blueprint of a body. So, you have a gene that is your blueprint. During conception, it is your genes and your partner's that form your baby's genes.

Now, if your child is autistic genetically, it is believed that the gene of your baby contains a change that has disrupted the gene's instructions.

This change can occur in two ways: changes that happened spontaneously at conception and changes that were inherited. So, some autistic people also have autistic children and some non-autistic people have autistic children.

You should also know that different kinds of gene mutations or changes are involved in autism spectrum disorder. And that is why the 'spectrum' is used to describe this condition.

It is a complex condition that manifests in varying degrees of severity. Hence, these genes do not even affect the child similarly.

Environmental factors. Besides genetic factors, research has shown that ecological factor causes autism, too.

The environment is defined medically as everything outside the human body that can alter one's health. Regarding this definition, the air, water, food, and even drugs are all-inclusive in the environmental factor.

So, when a baby is growing inside their mother's womb, the environmental factors that can influence the child's health include every element that surrounds the baby inside the uterus.

In further analysis, other environmental factors such as parent's age, family health history, medication during pregnancy, and various pregnancy complications were said to be part of the causes of autism.

In addition, a team of University of Chicago researchers concluded that exposing a fetus to toxins like pesticides can lead to a greater probability of your child being autistic.

Well, I believe that the pregnancy period is sensitive as it is the formative period of the baby. Plasticizers, prescription drugs, and environmental pesticides can affect the child.

Moreover, maternal smoking, drinking, and even use of thalidomide have been reported to accelerate the chances of your baby developing autism.

As much as all of these causes of autism has been supported by study, I believe there's nothing you would have done differently that would have changed your child's condition.

I was 39 when I gave birth to Peter, but we discovered he was autistic after fifteen months. Many people said that it was my age that influenced Peter's condition.

Instead of learning about my child and how I can help him enjoy his life, I spent a junk of time trying to understand why he was autistic, blaming myself for not mastering ovulation, and accusing my husband of not playing safe because we had stopped having children.

Years later, I realized I was wasting the time I had for early intervention to investigate what made my son autistic. If you are still at this point in your journey, take it from a woman who has been there-- it's not necessary. Focus on bringing up your wonderful child. Are you ready?

I want you to affirm, "I am a mother of an amazing child who happens to have autism"-Brenda Rothman.

KINDS OF AUTISM

I already mentioned that there are variant manifestations of autism in children. This section will discuss the five core types of autism. The essence of this information is to equip you with valuable insight into your child's unique strengths and challenges, enabling you to make informed decisions regarding early intervention and therapies.

Moreover, this information will help in networking with parents of autistic children more strategically because when you know the specific kind of autism your child is manifesting, you will be able to identify parents of children that manifest similar autistic conditions with your child and connect with them so as to share helpful tips together.

Asperger's Syndrome

This is also known as the level 1 spectrum disorder. Children with autism have above-average intelligence and verbal skills but struggle with social communication. They often exhibit one or more of the following symptoms:

- ✓ Inflexibility in thoughts and behavior
- ✓ Executive functioning problems
- ✓ Flat monotone speech
- ✓ Challenges in changing activities
- ✓ Difficulty interacting with peers

Rett Syndrome

This syndrome is noticed in infancy as it affects every aspect of the child. Statistics have shown that it is majorly seen in female children. Children with this syndrome can live an everyday life if their parents can provide support to allow the children to do what they enjoy. Some symptoms of this condition include:

- ✓ Loss of standard movement and coordination
- ✓ Breathing difficulties (in some cases)
- ✓ Speech and communication challenges

Childhood Dis-integrative Disorder (CDD)

CDD, which is also known as Heller's syndrome or disintegrative psychosis, is a neurodevelopmental problem that is characterized by delayed onset of developmental difficulties in language, social interaction, or motor skills. So, the children usually develop but hit a snag after age three to about ten.

The sad thing about CDD is that most parents are unaware of their children's autistic condition because there will be no autistic symptoms at first when they get to a certain age. This condition is common in boys, as nine out of every ten cases are boys. The symptoms include a child losing the following abilities:

- ✓ Acquired language

- ✓ Motor skills

- ✓ Social skills

- ✓ Toilet skills (if they have developed already)

Kanner's Syndrome

This syndrome was discovered in 1943 by a psychiatrist named Leo Kanner of Johns Hopkins University. He described this condition as one that involved an alert, attractive, and intelligent child but exhibited the following syndrome:

- ✓ Uncontrolled speech
- ✓ Obsession with handling objects
- ✓ Lack of emotional attachment to others
- ✓ Interaction challenges

Pervasive Developmental Disorder-Not otherwise specified (PDD-NOS)

This is the mild manifestation of autism, and the most common symptoms are social and language communication. A child with this kind of autism experiences delays in developing language and motor skills.

It is also referred to as sub-threshold autism because the individual does not display all the symptoms of autism. Understanding autism is the first stage of helping your child to live an independent life.

You have learned that autism is a condition that affects how a person perceives, communicates, and interacts with the world around them. Autism is caused by both genetic and environmental factors.

There are also five major kinds of autism and they include: Asperger's Syndrome, Kanner Syndrome, Childhood Dis-integrative Disorder (CDD), Rett Syndrome, and Pervasive Developmental Disorder-Not otherwise specified (PDD-NOS).

In the next chapter, I will show you the early signs of autism in a child. Many children are suffering not because they are autistic but because their parents treat them as neurotypical children and expect some pre-determined result.

How do you make a fish to crawl on the land and expect they do so? It is time for you to step into your child's shoe and communicate with them how they can understand.

TAKE HOME

1. Autism Spectrum Disorder ASD is a wide range of neurological conditions characterized by social skills, repetitive behaviors, and verbal and nonverbal communication.

2. ASD is said to be caused by genetic and environmental factors.

3. There is nothing you would have done differently to have a different child.

4. Children with autism can live an independent life if they are diagnosed early and helped.

CHAPTER TWO
EARLY SIGNS OF AUTISM

"I might hit developmental and societal milestones in a different order than my peers, but I can accomplish these small victories on my own time." - Haley Moss

No one knows when an autistic child is born. They don't hand you a certificate telling you, "Oh! He is autistic." Finding out if your child is autistic or not is entirely your business.

There is no single medical test like a blood test that diagnoses autism. And most importantly, you can't seek early intervention if you don't know the signs of autism. "So, how am I going to know if my son or daughter is autistic?"

That is why you must observe your children and occasionally check their developmental and social milestones. Some autistic children grow up without their parents noticing that they have autism because they are unaware of the early signs of autism.

Sadly, that ignorance is one of the worst things you can do to your child because if you cannot identify their condition, there's no way you will be able to help them. In this chapter, I will describe to you the wide range of autism symptoms that you can find in an autistic child.

Although the symptoms of autism are widely varied, they are majorly categorized into social communication and interaction difficulties and routines.

The Diagnostic and Statistical Manual Disorder has specially stated some of the symptoms that can help diagnose autism, and they are as follows:

- ✓ Difficulty with communication and interaction with other people

- ✓ Restricted interest and repetitive behaviors

- ✓ Symptoms that affect that person's ability to function in school work, and other areas of life.

Difficulty with communication and interaction

Communication is the act of giving and receiving information. Children can start communication with you from birth. They show you they are tired, awake, or hungry with different signals.

They are babies, and coming into the world is a big adventure for them. As a parent, your job is to learn to communicate with them the way they do as you teach them better ways to communicate.

An autistic child has communication difficulties compared to a non-autistic child, but they, too, can communicate if given the help they need. How do you help when you do not know they are having difficulties?

There's no way that's possible. At the end of this section, you will effortlessly identify difficulty with communication and interaction symptoms of autism and start an early intervention procedure for your child.

The communication signs in autistic children include the problems associated with the social communication and interaction of autistic children, and they have the following:

No Eye Contact

Eye contact is a nonverbal behavior that helps children communicate their interest and attention to you. It is also used to identify cues from you and respond accordingly.

However, you may notice that your child does not make eye contact. This symptom is often misinterpreted as disinterest at that moment, which could be accurate. Still, when this attitude persists, it is a signal that your child could need help to perform that communication skill.

According to the Diagnostic and Statistical Manual of Mental Disorders (DSM-5) published by the American Psychiatric Association, lack of eye contact is a symptom of autism.

Why do they behave this way?

Autistic children respond to eye contact differently from neurotypical children. Yale University scientists discovered that eye contact activities are prompted in different parts of the brain for autistic and non-autistic people after examining and comparing their brains.

Another research with an electroencephalogram revealed that children have a more robust response to a direct gaze than a downcast gaze. However, children with autism responded more strongly to sad looks than direct eye contact.

From the study above, children with autism don't like eye contact because of the following:

A. They lack the ordinary social motivation that prompts other children to make eye contact.
B. Paying attention to what someone is saying and maintaining eye contact simultaneously seems to be a herculean task for them.
C. They are unaware that making eye contact is a display of interest in what the person is saying.
D. Making and maintaining eye contact is an overwhelming sensory experience that they hope to avoid.

Moreover, some adults with autism have also explained why they avoid eye contact in several publications. Some of their opinions regarding eye contact are as follows:

- "Making eye contact is invasive, distracting and confusing."

- "Eye contact should be reserved for intimate relationship and people they trust."

- "Processing verbal information is more difficult when making eye contact."

- Others have said that eye contact is associated with negative physical symptoms such as dizziness, headaches, increased heart rate, nausea, pain, and tremors.

DELAY OR LACK OF JOINT ATTENTION

When a neurotypical child is playing or interacting with his peers or even playing by themselves, they have a common attribute of looking at the activities and simultaneously looking at you as a way of connecting with you, which is called joint attention.

In other words, a child has joint attention when they can conveniently be doing one thing and still be connected to you. This is a great communication skill in children as it is fundamental to developing more advanced communication skills.

An example of a child's joint attention display is when your child follows your gaze like you are showing them something, or when they are showing you something by pointing towards it and coordinating looks between you and an object, they want you to see.

Children with autism lack these vital developmental skills of sharing experience. Hence, they focus on one thing at a time and may never be able to share their experience with you. If you notice this sign in your child, you should pay more attention to know if they have autism.

NOT RESPONDING TO THEIR NAMES

Another communication sign that your child may be autistic is the inability to respond to their names, and this symptom is tested through the name test. This test was formulated by an assessment researcher at the University of California.

While this test in itself cannot diagnose autism, it can identify the developmental evidence of autism. In 2007, UC Davis Health Mind Institute researched the name test. The experiment was done with babies.

This name test was part of an ongoing autism research project. The babies were put into two different groups: the babies at high risk of autism and the controlled group (with no pre-determined risk of autism).

The first group of babies had older siblings who were autistic, while the second group didn't. All the infants were between the ages of 6 months to 12 months.

The experiment involved the researchers standing behind the babies during play and calling their names. If a baby doesn't respond, the researcher will wait a few seconds and call again. They called the names thrice for each child.

At 12 months, 100% of the children in the controlled group passed the test, while only 86% in the high autism-risk group passed. The researchers found no significant connection between children not responding to their names and autism diagnosis. At 24 months, more than 50% of the high-risk children who did not pass the name test were diagnosed with autism or other developmental conditions.

The conclusion of the study states that a 12-month-old child who rarely responds to their names could have a developmental delay or a condition called autism. However, they categorically stated that a name test alone cannot be used for diagnosis.

RARELY IMITATING YOUR ACTIONS

Usually, babies have a common attribute of mimicking the actions or sounds of people around them. It could be imitating your facial expressions or the sounds you make. Autistic children rarely copy the actions of others. You can also notice this in emotional responses. Babies tend to smile at people who smile at them and may even cry or feel concerned when they see their peers crying. A child with autism will hardly do that.

NEVER ENGAGES IN PRETEND PLAY

Pretend play is an integral part of the second year of a child's development. Children love to pretend to be dad, mom, uncle, or any character. It is funny how I still remember some of the pretend plays I engaged in as a child.

It was many decades ago. You might remember your experience if you tried to remember. It is famous for a baby girl to pretend to be a mother to a doll and gives her doll a bath.

A boy may pretend to be a father. But, autistic children don't engage in pretend play because they may encounter difficulties in generating new ideas and actions needed in pretend play.

Restricted interest and repetitive behaviors

The restricted interest is majorly a result of their sensory needs. These restricted interest births repetitive behaviors--what people may refer to as behavioral irregularity. We will discuss sensory needs and behavioral irregularities in autistic children.

Sensory Needs

The sensory system helps you perceive the environment's stimuli through sensory processing. Sensory processing is the process that involves the organization of the sensation from your background that makes it possible for your body to function effectively. Each autistic child is different and manifests a variety of sensory sensitivities.

Generally, two sensitivities are common in autistic children, including hypersensitivity and hypo-sensitivity.

Hypersensitivity refers to the over-responsiveness to body sensations like color, sounds, and smells. Children get overwhelmed by certain sounds, tastes, colors, etc. You can identify this sign in two ways.

Firstly, a child may practice sensory avoidance as a reflex to stimuli, such as pulling away from physical touch, refusing to wear certain clothes, covering their ears when there is noise, etc. Secondly, some children witness a negative behavioral change described as a 'meltdown.'

As its name implies, *hypo-sensitivity* is the under-responsiveness to various body sensations. This is the opposite of hypersensitivity. So, instead of the children engaging in sensory avoidance, they do 'sensory seeking.'

Children who suffer from this, move constantly, get attracted to noise and hardly notice when they get hungry, sick, or even in pain.

Behavioral Irregularity

A child with autism may have some behavioral irregularities. Your responsibility as a parent is to identify them and help them regulate such behaviors. In situations where you ignore these behaviors or treat them like tantrums, they may hurt themselves or the people around them. The behavioral difference manifests in two significant ways: stimming and meltdowns.

Stimming.

This refers to repetitive self-stimulatory acts. These behaviors are often not harmful, although they appear odd. For example, your child keeps jumping, hand flapping, all the time.

You can also notice that the child does things the same way, and doing it differently can upset them. A good example is seeing your child play with their toys the same way every time.

This may sound strange to first-time parents because they wonder; *does every child not do that?* No, children may play with the same toy but have a variety of play patterns. Imagine your child has a building block toy, and they build it the same way every time, and they get upset when the order is changed.

I remember working with a particular mother who lived in denial of her second child being autistic. She just told me that the child's developmental process is slower than her first's, and she was keen to find out what was wrong with him.

After a couple of weeks with me, I suspected he was autistic. One of the behavioral signs I noticed had to do with his building blocks game. He arranged it the same way and will bite anyone who tries to change the order, even his mother.

Sadly, when I tried to discuss my suspicion with his mom, it ended with an affirmation-- *"my child can never be autistic"*. I wasn't surprised; over the years, the label "autism" had been associated with some awful narratives.

Meltdowns

Autistic children experience what is called meltdowns. In this period, they lose control of themselves. It happens when they are emotionally overwhelmed. Meltdowns are manifested in various ways, as every child is different. During meltdowns, children could be crying, shouting, stimming, etc.

Although meltdowns have similar characteristics to tantrums, but they are not the same. You should never treat meltdowns like tantrums. Meltdowns are predictable because it is preceded by signs of stress.

Unlike an unpredictable tantrum, autistic children will display warning signs, which are referred to as rumblings. So, if you want to know if your child's behavior is a meltdown, you have to observe the situation.

Do you notice outward signs of distress? It may not even be so obvious. That's why you need to pay maximum attention. Some children could use their hands over the ears, while others may simply plead with you to let them leave the environment.

Another indicative difference between meltdown and tantrum is that tantrums are voluntarily done to obtain a goal. Children throw tantrums because they have perceived it as a way to get what they need.

A good example will be your child crying because they want you to give them ice cream. Maybe she reminded you about the ice cream you promised her a while ago, and you refused to keep your promise. So, she starts crying and maybe rolling on the floor. Children can be so manipulative, and that's part of our beautiful experience of watching our children grow.

No matter the level of aggression those children demonstrate, you can't refer to it as a meltdown and here is why. Autistic kids who experience meltdowns are genuinely distressed and not merely manipulating you to grant them their request.

Lastly, meltdowns differ from tantrums as meltdown comprises stimming while tantrums don't. When autistic children stim, they usually try to manage their emotions as they are on their way to being overwhelmed.

Symptoms That Can Affect a Person's Ability to Function in School Work, Work, And Other Areas of Life

The third classification of autism signs has to do with any pattern that affects the functionality of a person and some of those symptoms include:

Depression: People with depression may experience sadness, hopelessness, fatigue, difficulty concentrating, and changes in appetite or sleep. These symptoms can make it difficult to attend school or work, complete tasks, and maintain relationships.

Anxiety disorders: anxiety disorders can cause excessive fear, worry, and anxiety. People with anxiety disorders may also experience physical symptoms such as sweating, trembling, and shortness of breath. These symptoms can make it difficult to focus and concentrate, and can interfere with school work, work, and other activities.

Attention-deficit/hyperactivity disorder (ADHD): ADHD is a neurodevelopmental disorder that can cause difficulty paying attention, controlling impulsive behavior, and fidgeting or squirming. These symptoms can make it difficult to focus in school or work, and can lead to problems with relationships and self-esteem.

Substance use disorders: substance use disorders can cause problems in all areas of life, including school, work, relationships, and health. People with substance use disorders may experience cravings, withdrawal symptoms, and impaired judgment. These symptoms can make it difficult to function in school or work, and can lead to legal problems and financial difficulties.

Personality disorders: Personality disorders are a group of mental disorders that involve long-lasting patterns of thinking, feeling, and behaviors. These patterns can cause problems in relationships, work, and other areas of life.

People with personality disorders may experience difficulty controlling their emotions, relating to others, and making decisions.

These are just a few of the many disorders that can affect a person's ability to function in school work, and other areas of life. However, these symptoms are not exclusive to people with autism.

What age should Parent start watching out for the signs of autism?

There is no one definitive answer to this question, as the signs and symptoms of autism can vary from child to child. However, there are some general guidelines that parents can follow.

The American Academy of Pediatrics (AAP) recommends that all children be screened for autism at 18 months and again at 24 months of age. This screening can help identify children who may be at risk for autism and who may need further evaluation.

It is also important to remember that not all children with autism will exhibit all of these signs and symptoms. Some children may only have a few signs, while others may have many. If you are concerned about your child's development, it is always best to talk to your doctor.

In conclusion, knowing the early signs of Autism is important as it helps you to start asking the right people the right questions. From there, you can apply for a formal diagnosis and if your suspicion is confirmed, you can seek an early intervention, as it can make a huge difference.

Autism diagnosis should not be your worst nightmare. Many narratives of Autism that are crippling you with fear are false, and I hope we were able to trash some of them out of the window in this chapter.

Would you believe me if I told you that majority of the problems autistic individuals face is the society and not necessarily their condition? You may not, but it is true.

Knowing your child is wired differently at the early stage of his developmental life should be a relief. So, you will have to stop guessing and do what you have to do.

The question now is, what do we have to do? After identifying the signs of Autism in a child, then what? In the next chapter, I will share the information no one has ever told you about how special your child is.

TAKE HOME

- Each autistic child is different and manifests a variety of sensory sensitivities: hypersensitivity and hypo-sensitivity
- Parenting does not cause Autism, but positive parenting is the best support an autistic child can get.
- Autism is not an illness; rather, it is a behavioral condition, and it is by observing the symptoms that a professional can deduce that a child is autistic.
- Autism is diagnosed based on symptoms like communication and social challenges, narrow interests, repetitive behaviors, and difficulties in school or work. These are outlined in the Diagnostic and Statistical Manual Disorder.

CHAPTER THREE
ACCEPTING YOUR AUTISTIC CHILD

"Autism is part of my child; it's not everything he is. My child is so much more than a diagnosis."

Accepting your child is the being of every parenting journey, and the funny thing is that the moment you accept your child in any kind of condition, everything becomes easier to handle. This chapter is going to expound on the why and how to accept your autistic child.

The truth is there is always a struggle to accept your autistic child especially when you have a negative outlook of autism. I met Maria two years ago; when her little, energetic son was diagnosed with autism.

Maria was pained that she wished it was a dream. I remember doing the most foolish thing ever in my career as a neurodivergent specialist. Can you guess what I did? I said, "You just need to accept him for who he is. You know this isn't a death sentence..."

Before I could utter more words that I thought were soothing, this woman who found everything I said stupid and unnecessary stopped me. She was pissed. She made me understand I had no right to tell her what to do and how to feel until I had an autistic child with no partner to share responsibility with.

When her shaky voice told her story. My mouth remained zipped while I fixed my gaze on her. Maria had just decided to go to college and pursue a career she had always wanted before her son was confirmed to be autistic.

After she vented, I realized she felt alone, confused, disappointed, and ashamed that she had an autistic child. Maybe I should ask you if you have similar feelings because you were so excited about having your child until you discovered that he or she was different.

What changed?

Now, you are disappointed. You fear that you may never get the opportunity to live some fantasies you had as an expectant mother. You're ashamed to have a child with several meltdowns in a week, making people label them "abnormal."

In this section, I will tell you why it is essential to accept your child, what it means to do so, and how you can do that. However, this chapter is not here to tell you what you **MUST** do-- the mistake I made with Maria.

I am here to help you and not insist on what you should do with your child. Fifteen years ago, I was where you are now. I was sad, worried, angry. It was the worst day of my life. Then, information about autism was not readily at our fingertips like it is now.

Nobody told me about accepting my child. Everyone kept on telling me how to fix my son. They made me believe he was sick and would never have a normal life. I was tortured with the thought that he will always be a dependent.

I can't really tell the whole story. The worst thing about my son's situation was that, his autism symptoms were not mild. It degenerated continuously. I felt like my beautiful child was stolen and another child I considered undesirable was used for replacement.

But when I accepted my son, I connected with my child, and everything turned around. I feel special to have such a unique child that even if I can make him non-autistic at the snap of my fingers, I would never snap them because I have grown to love him. Do you want to love your child unconditionally? Are you tired of being ashamed of being a mother or father? Then, I am inviting you to accept your child.

What does accepting your child mean?

Accepting your child means acknowledging that your child is wired differently and being grateful to have them. Accepting your child may not happen overnight; it is a progressive journey. This journey of acceptance takes longer time because our society hardly accept it.

The stories about autism are majorly negative and affect how we look at our children. The society that raised you and me places so much emphasis on conditional acceptance.

If you are not behaving in some specific ways and they don't see your external display of awesomeness, they don't see you as someone worthy of endorsement or acceptance and this is ridiculous.

But it is funnier how the non-acceptance of autistic children in society is extended to their parents. I am not just criticizing the society; I am criticizing everyone who has such mentality that people are not worthy of acceptance if they were not born a certain way.

You didn't choose the way you were born either did I. So, why should you be accepted or rejected just because of how you were born? It makes no sense to me.

Maybe if Peter didn't come into my life fifteen years ago; I would have been part of the society I am talking about. You must understand that society is not an open space; you and I are the society.

It is our individualized mindsets that makes the opinion of the society. Listen to this, if you want to succeed in accepting your child, I will tell you the truth: society shouldn't matter.

I will show you how to accept your child but before then, let's talk about some lies people have talked about autism. Discussing these misconceptions will help you accept your child because many times that is what is keeping you from doing so.

MISCONCEPTIONS OF AUTISM

Over half of the world's population has heard about Autism, but the number of misinformed people is unbelievable. Autism has many false narratives. Initially, I was caught in this web of misinformation, and it affected me so much, especially in accepting my son.

For the sake of this book, we will focus on ten common misconceptions, including the ones I had.

1. **Autism is an illness**. This is the most popular misconception about Autism, and I think it is what begat panic in the lives of many parents. They always feel sad or terrible about having to parent a sick child.

I will not pretend as if I didn't feel this way after my last child was diagnosed autistic. I thought I had a broken child that would distract me from hitting my career goal.

I dwelled in frustration all day, and I remember how I transferred aggression to everybody around me. I agree that some autistic children can be a handful, since autism manifestations can be mild or extreme, but the word 'sick' does not fit into this concept. Your child is healthy.

I hope you know that autism cannot be cured with drugs and that diagnosis isn't determined by doing some regular lab test. This is because autism is a behavioral condition, and it is by observing the symptoms that a professional can deduce that a child is autistic.

2. **Autism is caused by vaccines.** This was the most painful, widespread lie I have heard about autism, and this is why I think so. This false narrative will alter some lives because some people will avoid vaccines to prevent autism but end up exposing their children to different diseases.

The sad thing is that many people who believe this will continuously tell these deceptive stories without even knowing they are causing harm.

Interestingly, I learned recently that the myth of vaccines causing Autism was born out of a famous 1990 research report that managed to connect some vaccines to autism.

Although this faulty report was later debunked as it lacked scientific evidence and even the medical professional who masterminded the research was stripped of his license, this story has not stopped spreading like wildfire globally.

3. **Autism is an emerging pandemic**. I have also observed that the increasing number of diagnosed autism cases has fueled the false news of autism becoming a pandemic. Autism cannot be an epidemic. An epidemic is an outbreak of a contagious disease that spreads rapidly.

This misconception is like comparing the COVID pandemic to autism but making it seem that children are mostly affected. I know that in the last two decades, the number of children that have been diagnosed has tripled.

Still, I firmly believe that this is a case of people paying more attention to what has always been there following the increase in awareness and not necessarily an autism era.

4. **All Autistic people have a savant skill**. I believed this particular one for many years. In some of my writings, you may still hear me share my stories about some exceptional abilities of autistic individuals, which is not false.

Peter draws so beautifully and sings even better, but he does not have those skills because he is autistic. Autistic children can be talented, but the misconception comes in when you say ALL autistic children are born with a unique ability to do something extraordinary and exceptional. But in the real sense, it is a small population of autistic people who are gifted with some special skills, which is even the same as the non-autistic population.

It is also worth mentioning that in my years of studying autism, I have realized that autistic people most times have concentrated attention on one single field or topic, and over time, they become so good at that thing that people will randomly label it "a talent," but they weren't born with such ability.

This can happen to anyone; if you focus on a particular topic, you become extraordinarily good at it, but you can't attribute it to a talent from birth.

5. **Another funny and annoying misconception is that autistic children don't experience emotions.** Hence, they cannot have friendships or love relationships. I have interacted with autistic children and adults and can confidently tell you this is a myth.

Autistic children are capable of feeling all kinds of emotions that a non-autistic person feels. They get happy, sad, angry. I understand autistic individuals are wired differently, affecting their communication and social interaction abilities.

Hence, people unfamiliar with this uniqueness tend to label them emotionless. In addition, the neurodevelopmental condition poses a challenge in interpreting other people's emotions, body language, and expressions. However, this should never be mistaken for unwillingness or disinterest to connect and socialize.

6. **Autistic people have an intellectual disability and can't speak.** This myth is predominant among people with little or no knowledge about Autism. Autism is not an intellectual disability. I explained earlier that Autism has variant manifestations and that no two autistic children are the same.

While some autistic children communicate verbally, others don't. Some autistic children have a higher IQ than others. Hence, you should not generalize one autistic situation you saw.

7. **Autism is a child developmental thing you grow out of it as time progresses**. Autism is a lifelong condition that you don't grow out of. You don't cure autism because it is not a sickness. Even the therapy sessions are not designed to take autism away; instead, they help an autistic person with a specific life area, like developing new skills or a variant of social skills and improving their daily life.

So, if you have a child with Autism, you are not seeking trans-formative therapy that will change him or her into a non-autistic person; you are investing the time and resource to make sure he or she have an everyday life like everyone else by understanding their unique autism manifestation and helping them.

8. **Autistic people cannot learn**. This is similar to the misconception about intellectual disability. Still, I decided to tackle this alone because it is kind of famous, and one of the myths that worries parents the most. I do not know how else to say it, but believe me, it is a lie.

Whether Autism or not, our learning capacities are different. Everyone wondered why I was not as bright as my parents in elementary school, but I was one of the brightest students in college. Everyone at some point can be flagged to have learning irregularities if their teachers do not understand their learning peculiarities.

A child with Autism can learn anything at all. However, each person is different from another. So, some autistic children will require more understanding, method adaptation, and therapy to achieve some levels of learning; others may not. This is why professional treatment is available to improve the learning process of autistic persons at their own speed and rate.

9. **Autism is caused by bad parenting**. The first time I heard this, I felt terrible. It was a couple sharing their parenting journey with their nonverbal autistic teenager. I felt terrible for them because people made them feel like they were awful parents, and that's why their child developed autism.

I made them understand that there is no evidence to support the claim that parenting contributes to having an autistic child. When I did my further research, I was able to establish a link between this offensive myth and the refrigerator mother hypothesis of the 1950s.

The summary of this theory is that cold mothers emotionally traumatize their children to the extent that they develop Autism.

Although this theory has been scientifically debunked, the story has not stopped spreading. Meanwhile, parenting does not cause Autism, but parenting is the best support an autistic child can get.

10. **Autistic children are the most violent kind of children.** In my opinion, no child should be made to believe that he is more damaging than his peers because he is autistic. That's a stigma that no child deserves to live with, mainly because it is untrue.

Some autistic children are violent, while others are not. However, throwing tantrums as kids is not only displayed by autistic children. In fact, when an autistic child expresses violence, especially when he is not getting what he wants.

Chances are that he is being violent because he has not learned other coping mechanisms. Some children may just be reacting to their sensory needs, and once that is taken care of, they never get violent.

Why is accepting your autistic child necessary?

1. It helps to boost your mental health. Stop ignoring your mental health because it matters. You may experience frequent emotional stress that leaves you exhausted and unable to support yourself and your child if you refuse or delay accepting your child.

2. It is the best step to helping your child. We have already established that an autistic child is not broken yet different and, as such, needs help to learn new skills. You are responsible for supporting them and can't do that efficiently without accepting your child. Are you ready to accept your child? Below are the steps I took, and I am sure you can intentionally receive your child by following them.

How can I accept my child?

1. **Give yourself some accolades**. I love to start with the fact that I am proud of you. None of us specifically asked for autistic children, or most of us never knew what autism was before the arrival of our babies, and we have been putting effort into giving them the best parenting there is. That alone is worth celebrating regardless.

2. **You need to accept yourself first**. Taking care of your autistic child starts with loving yourself and permitting yourself to be beautiful, unique, lovable, and all that good stuff.

Someone told me sometime last year that this step was just a cliché, and I pitied him because he had no idea how it can help him be a wonderful father to his daughter.

We talk to ourselves the exact same way we consider rude and demeaning. Some of us whisper negative words to ourselves behind closed doors.

"You are not a loser. You are not behind. You are not a failure. It is not your fault that your child has autism. Shower some love on yourself.

And I must remind you that setting goals, having dreams, and having great relationships is super-amazing, but that is not the standard for loving yourself. Learn to love yourself unconditionally.

Practice affirmation, self-care, and mindful compassion for yourself. I watch parents who are loveless try to love their children. I hope you know you can't give what you don't have.

3. Focus on what you love about your child. I start and end almost every conversation with a parent to an autism child with this question-- "what do you love about your child?" I started practicing that ever since I discovered how therapeutic that question is.

You should pause here and take a few minutes to reminisce about what you love about your child. Is it the way they smile, how they run and fall, or the sounds they make? The more you focus on the beautiful things about your child, the more you can cut off the negative thoughts that hover around your child's condition in your head.

Whether you like it or not, if you refuse to accept your child, they feel it, and may never heal. There's something about energy that you cannot manipulate. Accepting your child, the way they are is building the muscle you need to be the best parent you can be.

Remember that the core of parenting a child, whether autistic or not, is to be there for them always and make sure that they are aware that you are always there for them.

POST DIAGNOSIS EXPERIENCE

I have met hundreds of parents who had just gotten their positive autism diagnosis for their children, and I will say they are not always okay.

They are worried, scared, and sad about the whole thing; some even live in denial. Today, I won't be talking to you about the thousands of parents I have met; I will speak to you about yourself.

Where are you presently? Are you still suspecting, or have you gotten a formal diagnosis of your child? Whatever stage you are in is fine, and I hope you do the right thing in this period.

You wish that your child was a typical child. You deserved a 'normal' child, you always say. You don't even care how much I want to tell you about accepting your child because you still prefer your baby without any 'funny' behavior.

In fact, you still don't even believe all the misconceptions I have explained to you because you believe I am just trying to comfort you in this 'tragic' circumstance. I understand this is what is going through your mind. And I want to let you know that it is normal.

However, there are things I want you to always remember as you go through this season. These nuggets I want to share with you do not blur the fact that your child has autism, but they will help you open your mind to understand the situation of things that will form your reaction.

Take your time to breathe. You can live your everyday life with autistic children and even experience most, if not all, of your expectations, but I understand that you don't know that as a fact.

I learned about most of what I am writing in this book, because I was constantly researching and training my son and my other children. So, it is okay to be overwhelmed. It is okay to believe all those false autism stories you have heard since childhood.

However, you shouldn't always stay here. After taking the time to think things through, you need to take a step. What is the action you should take?

Gather information by reading, asking questions, attending relevant events, and networking with fellow parents, but in all you do, don't allow the autism diagnosis to intimidate you.

You can feel depressed for a while, but just for some time. All you need is information to help you handle the situation, and you will be fine, I promise.

Your child was not switched. Often, after an autism diagnosis, most parents feel like their babies have been exchanged. Do you now look at your child through the lens of pity, burden, or worry? If you do, you need to stop it.

He or she is still the sweet baby you fell in love with; nothing has changed except how you see them now, and it is possible to change that again. You need to take it one step after the other.

You are not the reason why your child has autism. There is only one thing that you could have done differently that would have prevented you from having an autistic child. Do you want to know what it is? It is not having a child at all.

In as much that you feel embarrassed when your child has a meltdown in public, and you regret coming out that day, they are still yours. People stare at you, and you instantly feel guilt, know that it is not your fault.

You may even hear whispers that your child simply needs discipline or that you are not just a good parent. Trust me when I say; I know how that feels, but the question is: Will you allow people who don't know anything about the situation to dictate how you think? If no, then, focus on your child rather than what people think.

The diagnosis should not change the trajectory of your life. I spoke to a friend recently, and she explained how her daughter's autism changed her life. She married a young, ambitious man like herself in her mid-twenties.

She was a dentist. When she found out her first daughter was autistic, she was already pregnant with her second child. And her second child was also autistic. It was burdensome to her. She stopped working and stopped dreaming.

She said she was going in circles for over seven years of her life. She described these periods as the most confused and horrible experience of her life. Today, she is an autism professional, but that was not what she started out to do.

Listen, never allow autism diagnosis to steal your joy. You can dwell on your fears or choose to be optimistic. Having an autistic child will not squeeze happiness out of your household if you don't allow it.

Finally, **you are not alone and should never feel that way.** Immediately after the diagnosis, especially if you live in denial, you may have frequent depressing thoughts.

You may be tempted to feel you are the only mother or father with an autistic child because people around you are unfamiliar with autism.

Sometimes, pals may stop coming around you after you share the diagnosis with them. It is normal. It is not their fault they are avoiding you; maybe you would have done the same if you were in their shoes.

What should you do rather than chasing friends that are not comfortable around your home is to find parents who have autistic children, too.

Joining an online support group is a great way to connect with such parents and locate the ones who live closer to you. You can also search for recreational places, where you can take your child, and I am sure you will make new friends there.

7 Things You Should Research About in Post Diagnosis

Educate yourself about autism: The more you know about autism, the better equipped you will be to help your child. There are many resources available to help you learn about autism, including books, websites, and support groups.

Get your child's insurance coverage in place: Many autism treatments and therapies are not covered by insurance, so it is important to understand your child's coverage and what treatments are available. You may need to advocate for your child to get the treatment they need.

Find the right school for your child: Not all schools are equipped to meet the needs of children with autism. Do your research and find a school that has a good reputation for working with children with autism.

Build a strong support network: Raising a child with autism can be challenging, so it is important to have a strong support network in place. This could include family, friends, therapists, and other parents of children with autism.

Take care of yourself: It is important to take care of yourself, both physically and emotionally. Raising a child with or without autism can be stressful, so it is important to find ways to relax and de-stress.

Therapy and treatment: There are many different types of therapy and treatment available for children with autism. Some of the most common types include behavioral therapy, speech therapy, and occupational therapy.

Socialization: Children with autism often need help learning how to socialize with others. There are many different ways to help your child with this, such as enrolling them in social skills groups or playing with other children in your community.

Communication: Children with autism may have difficulty communicating their needs and wants. There are many different ways to help your child communicate, such as using sign language, picture cards, or augmentative and alternative communication (AAC) devices.

Raising a child with autism can be a challenge in a society like ours, hence why you need the correct information and a good support system. Don't allow the society to stop you from embracing your child and taking the necessary actions to make sure they reach their full potential.

TAKE HOME

- Autistic children are capable of feeling all kinds of emotions that a non-autistic person feels.
- Focus on what you love about your child

- Autistic children are the most violent kind of children

- Autistic children can be a handful since autism manifestations can be mild or extreme, but the word 'sick' does not fit into this concept.

CHAPTER FOUR

POSITIVE REINFORCEMENT

"If they can't learn the way we teach, we teach them the way they learn." - Dr. O. Ivar Lovaas

Millions of children have learned new skills and unlearned problem behavior with positive reinforcement. In this chapter, I will describe the positive reinforcement strategy, the benefits of this learning strategy, why some people detest it, and, of course, give you practical instructions to help it work for your child.

Positive reinforcement is a strategy that is based on the idea that *all behaviors have consequences*. Whether as a child or as an adult, there is a consequence for your behaviors. It doesn't matter if we observe these consequences or not.

Let me give you a funny example: You remember that you did something before you conceived your child.

Although, I wasn't in the room or wherever it happened, but I know you did something, and the consequence of your action is the bundle of joy you call your child. It doesn't matter whether you adopted; what counts is that you took one action or actions that gave you a child.

In the same light, your children have different types of behaviors that attract different consequences. If your child is playing with his peers, the result may be that they feel good.

Since that consequence is something, they like, they will play often. Feeling good is a positive reinforcement because it increases the probability of the child playing.

In other words, a positive reinforcer involves the type of consequence that increases the probability of the child repeating the behavior when introduced immediately after a behavior is performed. I hope you see how this strategy can help your child acquire new skills or strengthen old ones.

WHY DO PEOPLE DETEST THIS STRATEGY?

We are all different and, hence, perceive things differently. Some people don't think positive reinforcement is a suitable learning method because they see it as coercion or bribery.

In 2020, one of the parents I discussed positive reinforcement thought it was a form of bribery. Although that was not the first time, I heard that school of thought, I really understood her fears, and I remember after that call, I did more research into her concerns.

She told me, *Sharon, I want to help my child more than you want me to. But I need to be logical. Why do I have to reward my child for doing the basic things he has to do?*

If autism is not as big a deal as you preach, why can't I just train my child like a non-autistic child and allow him to become who he was created to be? I explained that there is a difference between bribery and positive reinforcement.

Bribery happens when an individual is rewarded for an unethical behavior. In a child's upbringing, bribing your child happens in the middle of an undesirable behavior.

Maybe your child is throwing tantrums, and you offer him candy to make him keep quiet, but this is not what positive reinforcement is all about.

Let me ask you: "Have you ever been rewarded at your job?" For example, your KPIs may have surpassed the month's goal, and you were given a reward for appreciation and encouragement to continue doing an excellent job. Will you tell me you were bribed?

My sister got an annual profit-sharing bonus equivalent to her four months' salary because her performance at work was rated excellent by key stakeholders at the company.

So, tell me. Was she bribed to do her job? No. Was she motivated to continue being a great employee? Yes. If you don't see anything wrong with someone giving you a reward to encourage you to perform a particular task, you should not see positive reinforcement as a bad idea.

In addition, positive reinforcement is not coercion. Coercion occurs when an individual is compelled by force to do something without considering the individual's desires.

Positive reinforcement only crosses the line when it becomes a negative reinforcement and at that point, it is no longer positive reinforcement.

Naturally, we learn by coercion. If as a child, you touched a hot stove, you would never go near a stove- -and sometimes, you wouldn't even care if it was cold or hot. Right? But is this what positive reinforcement mean? No.

When teaching special needs children new skills, we care so much about the children's welfare throughout the process and not merely the end result.

We don't want socially active children with scars and mental damage that they have to live with.

This is why positive reinforcement is preferred, even though it takes longer time and a more significant financial budget. Positive reinforcement rewards a child for a desired behavior or motivates them to continue it.

WHY YOU SHOULD USE POSITIVE REINFORCEMENT

With positive reinforcement, you can help your child learn or improve the following:

A. **Functional life skills** like toilet skills can be taught by attaching reinforcement to proper toilet behavior.

B. **Verbal communication skills**: Some autistic children can be encouraged to communicate verbally with positive reinforcement. A little boy from Macomb County Kaufman Children's Center regained his verbal skills through this strategy.

According to his parents, he suffered severe apraxia, which means that although his brain could form the words to speak, he lacked the motor ability to talk about a comment.

His parents had lost hope; they had already begun to accept the possibility that he was a non-verbal autistic child, but positive reinforcement, alongside other strategies, made him gain his verbal communication skills.

C. **Non-verbal communication skills** such as facial expressions, gestures, eye contact, and so on, which are essential in communication, can be improved with positive reinforcement.

D. **Academic performance**: Reading, writing, math, and other academic tasks can be a bit more challenging for some autistic children, but when rewarded, they develop interest and learn to do better.

E. **Adaptive learning skills** like motor and self-help skills are essential for your child's development.

F. This method can enhance your **children's social interaction skills**.

G. Positive reinforcement is also instrumental in **reducing or eliminating undesirable behavior** by reinforcing an alternative behavior.

HOW TO USE POSITIVE REINFORCEMENT

Beyond the definition of positive reinforcement, knowing how to efficiently practice this strategy to achieve the desired result is essential.

You should also know that some misconceptions about this learning method were born out of a wrong application of the learning process. Below are the steps to follow when using positive reinforcement:

1. Identify the skill you want to teach your child or the behavior you want to encourage. Before considering positive reinforcement, you might have identified some problem behaviors or your child's lack of necessary skills.

Decide the reinforcement you want to leverage to teach them the skill. The type of reinforcement that works is not anything your child likes but something they really love.

When you use a reinforcement they love, the child can even do something they don't want to do just because of the reinforcement. Sometimes, it may be challenging to select a reinforcement for your child.

A great tip is to consider what they do during their free time. Some good examples include snacks, toys, games on their tablet, cartoon time, cuddle time with mummy, and so on.

When selecting a reinforcement, make sure it is something you can provide. Don't worry about choosing the wrong one; there's no right or wrong reinforcement, although a better one could exist. Remember that you can change a reinforcement if it doesn't work well.

2. Decide the situation or the task that must be completed for the reinforcement. The behavior will have to be the one you want to teach the child or encourage the child to do more.

You will need to communicate this to your child, and depending on the child's communication abilities, you will find different ways to tell them about their subsequent rewards.

While some parent communicates to their children verbally accompanied with sign language, other parents use some graphical representation to communicate with their children what they will get at the end of a specific activity.

Another suitable method of sharing this with your children is introducing the reward in the task process to build their expectations. After a couple of times when they have mastered the order, you won't need to bring the prize in the middle of their task.

3. Make sure to set up a conducive environment to enable the completion of their task. The environment doesn't only refer to the couch and table; every external part that affects the child is an element of his

environment and should be optimized to his comfort.

5. Ensure you practice immediate reinforcement. Autistic children have poor language skills, which makes it challenging to understand delayed reinforcement.

Imagine that your five-year-old child had to do her homework every day to get weekly reinforcement; if that child is autistic, she will not be able to follow through because she will not find it easy to associate the delayed reinforcement with the task she has been assigned.

5. Moderate the reinforcement as time goes on. As time passes, you will notice that your child has developed the desired skill, and you must strategically moderate the reinforcement.

For example, you are trying to reinforce the behavior of your child cleaning their rooms. You might offer them cookies when they arrange their clothes and a thirty-minute tablet time when they sweep their room.

After a month, when you notice that they consistently keep their room clean, you can only offer tablet time when they arrange their clothes and sweep their room. That way, you are trying to monitor and moderate the reinforcement.

COMMON POSITIVE REINFORCEMENT MISTAKES MADE AND HOW TO CORRECT THEM

1. Some parents have high demands with low reinforcement. As parents, we ought to have demands from our children. However, you must know when your demand is high, especially for a special need child.

You may not know your demand is a big deal, but here is the logic. If your child is not performing your demand consistently, there is something wrong. In figuring out what is wrong, always consider the option of lowering the bar.

For example, if shower time is a terrible time for your child, consider breaking down the process and this will help you find out what is frustrating them and tackle it.

But when you demand your children to perform their full morning routine of bathing, brushing, greeting, eating and offering them just a high five as a reinforcement.

You are simply demanding too much with little reinforcement and not even dealing with what may be disturbing them. In the long run, this approach never works.

I suggest lowering your demands and increasing reinforcement each time. Then, you can stick to the option that works best.

2. Reinforcing undesirable behavior without knowing it. A reinforcer could be anything so far as your child needs it. I read a story of a little boy with autism who habitually threw his food away regularly.

His nanny would yell at him and lock him up in his room for thirty minutes each time he threw his food away. Guess what happened? The behavior multiplied.

His nanny thought she was punishing the little child and was probably hoping he would desist from such acts, but he didn't. The nanny was unknowingly reinforcing an undesirable behavior.

My advice is when you notice an undesired behavior, especially one that is increasing, try to identify its reinforcer and cut it off; I will explain more of this in the subsequent chapter.

3. Removing reinforcement too quickly. As I explained, adjusting your support from time to time is essential. As time passes, your baby can continue his new behavior without reinforcer.

However, cutting off the reinforcement too early is a mistake. If you do so, you will be surprised to see your child stop the new behavior. The question I often get when I talk about this, is, how long should we consider?

To answer this, you should remember that every child is different. Some children will require only a few months, while others will take longer. I advise reducing the reinforcement bit by bit and not taking everything off at once.

4. Trying to simultaneously teach your child all the skills he lacks. Take it one skill at a time or a set of related skills per time.

There are other mistakes people make while implementing this strategy. Still, we covered many of them in how to implement positive reinforcement, so I won't be repeating it.

POSITIVE REINFORCEMENT: How to teach your child how to brush her teeth

1. Choose the right toothbrush and toothpaste: The regular toothbrush and toothpaste may not be a good idea for your child, especially if they have oral sensitivity. A toothbrush with soft bristles will be a good choice.

You should explore children-friendly flavor kinds of toothpaste. If you use mint toothpaste, your child might not like brushing with a bitter or burning sensation, making them hate it. You can ask for suggestions from your doctor or your support group.

2. Help them to know the brushing timing: My nephew, although not autistic, brushes her teeth in 30 seconds whenever he is in the bathroom alone. He just licks up the toothpaste and rinses the brush. But we don't want that. Some children's toothbrushes sing or blinks lights to indicate brushing timing. You can leverage that innovation. if your child is not triggered by them, you can even install a timer in their bathroom if it is possible.

3. Teach them the steps of tooth brushing: If your child has learned how to imitate actions, teach them how to brush using imitation. In addition, you can also recite the steps of brushing in a rhythmic tone.

4. Introduce a reward: A simple hug and a peck on the forehead can make your child brush willingly.

5. Build a routine: You can add brushing into your kid's schedules by putting it on their wall posters or calendars and attaching a specific time to it.

TAKE HOME

- Positive reinforcer involves the type of consequence that increases the probability of the child repeating the behavior when introduced immediately after a behavior is performed.
- Reinforcement is not coercion or bribery.
- Sometimes, parents reinforce undesirable behavior without knowing it.

CHAPTER FIVE
EXTINCTION

"Though devastating at first. Autism isn't the end of the world. It is the beginning of a whole new one."

All your child's negative behaviors can be stopped if you read and practice this chapter. The extinction strategy involves removing an existing reinforcement of a specific behavior (usually a negative behavior). This strategy aims to help the child unlearn the problem behavior they have.

Imagine a child banging on the door anytime he wants to go outside. If a parent or caregiver opens the door for him, whenever he does that, they are reinforcing that habit even though they think it is unacceptable. Parents unconsciously encourage problem behavior without knowing it.

If you want to help your child to stop an undesirable character, identify these characters and the reinforcement of those characters. Then remove the reinforcement to discourage the behavior, that's what extinction entails.

In this chapter, I will identify critical situations where extinction can be used, the merits and demerits of the extinction method, and practical steps to using extinction to eliminate problem behaviors in your autistic child.

Where is Extinction needed?

1. **Eliminate problem behaviors**: Most autistic children develop problem behaviors because they use those behaviors to get access to something they want but can't communicate properly.

For example, if your child needs attention but can't communicate it, they may do anything that makes you give them attention, even if it is negative behavior.

These undesirable behaviors can be frustrating sometimes, but I need you to know that your children are not exhibiting those characteristics because they want to get on your nerves. Rather, they use the easiest way to communicate something to you.

Now that you know why their problem behaviors are increasing, you need to remove the reinforcement so they will stop being motivated to engage in such behaviors.

The idea behind this strategy is that; when the child notices that their action is no longer functional or no longer gives them what they are looking for, they will stop.

2. **Wrapping up positive reinforcement**: I told you earlier that you will keep adjusting the reinforcement while using the positive reinforcement to teach your child to perform a task till it gets to the point where they can accomplish that task without a reinforcement attached, and at that point, you will need to eliminate the reinforcement but retain the behavioral change.

Imagine that your child's reinforcement for doing schoolwork is a bar of chocolate. Would you give him a bar of chocolate every day of his life? No. So, extinction is used when you want to detach reinforcement from a behavioral change.

3. **Sensory Regulation**: When we discussed the sensory system, I mentioned that some children with autism experience hypersensitivity and hypo-sensitivity. The children often employ some coping mechanisms you may want to discontinue.

For example, if a child is excited about playing with the light switch, you can disconnect the light so that there is no light when they turn on the switch.

Removing that particular sensory trigger is the only way to effectively do this. This process is referred to as automatic reinforcement. When you do this, your child loses interest in playing with the light switch because it no longer provides a function.

Merits of Extinction Method

You should consider using extinction method to teach your child because of the following:

1. It reduces problem behaviors in your autistic child.

2. Beyond weakening problem behaviors, it promotes positive behaviors, when an alternative behavior is introduced.

3. There's a high probability of communication improvement as the negative behaviors are

discontinued, and alternative communication skills are explored which may foster social and language skill development.

4. This method has proven to help parents and caregivers achieve independence, leading to greater self-regulation.

5. It is also a way to help the child reduce stress, but this is usually at the end of the day when the problem behavior has diminished.

Demerits Of Extinction Method

Extinction method have some disadvantages and they include the following:

1. The occurrence of Extinction burst: An extinction burst refers to the temporary increase of the target problem behavior during extinction.

Although the period of extinction burst is worrisome and frustrating, you should not stop implementing this strategy except on one condition--that your child is causing self-harm or harm others around them.

2. Increase in aggression: Children with autism will react in different ways to diverse training methods, and therapies. Some children become aggressive when the extinction method is used.

As a parent, you should evaluate the level of aggression. Describe his specific attitudes or even create a video so you can share it with the professional you are working with to get some helpful advice.

3. The risk of emotional stress is high, especially when practiced with no reinforcement (as it should be). Withholding support from a child can make them undergo emotional stress, and this is not what we want. The way to tackle this is by introducing an alternative behavior while eliminating the problem behavior.

4. Spontaneous Recovery is another demerit of Extinction. It refers to the reappearance of a previously extinguished behavior after some time. This often occurs if the initial learning is partially forgotten. But the good news is that the behavior is always temporary and weaker than the initial time before extinction method was implemented.

Practical steps to using Extinction with your autistic child.

1. It starts with a functional behavioral assessment (FBA): FBA means carefully examining problem behavior to identify the cause or function of the child's behavior. The main goal of FBA is to determine why the child engages in problem behavior.

2. Choose an intervention strategy: So, let's say you want to use the extinction method to help a child stop an undesired behavior. You must remember that every child is different and might react differently, so it is good to moderate this process.

3. Withdraw the reinforcement: Now that you have decided to use extinction, you will remove the reinforcement. While implementing this learning strategy, it makes sense to work with others like older kids, caregivers, nannies, or teachers.

I have seen parents implementing learning methods that teachers know nothing about. This negligence will change your child's behavior only at home and not generalized.

4. Consider introducing an alternative to the problem behavior: In my years of helping parents understand their children and giving them all the support, they can, I have noticed that this part of teaching children how to communicate better while simultaneously trying to eliminate a problem behavior is not popular.

If you don't want him banging on the door when they want to go outside, tell him what he should do instead. You may want him to talk to you, make eye contact, or point to the door.

As we already established, extinction can be uncomfortable for the learner and parents. Suppose your child is becoming aggressive during extinction (especially when it involves self-injury or causing harm to people around him).

In that case, you should consider reviewing the extinction method. I have learned to manage that outburst by introducing an additional procedure like reinforcing an alternative behavior.

HOW TO TEACH YOUR CHILD TOILET SKILLS WITH EXTINCTION.

Scenario: Your seven-year-old doesn't wipe his butt after using the toilet and never remembers to flush. Let's say you want to teach your child this personal care skill.

You have tried talking to them, but it didn't work. And you just realized that scolding them after an improper toileting even reinforces the act. So, how do you leverage extinction to teach them this skill?

Objectives: You must start your journey with a specific goal in mind. Let's say our objectives are:

1. To ensure that Johnny cleans himself properly after using the toilet and flushes the toilet as well.

What is the problem behavior?

1. Not cleaning their butts

2. Not flushing the toilet

What is the function of the problem behavior for your child?

1. Not Flushing: Getting attention from mummy

2. Not cleaning: Getting attention from mummy

10 practical steps to take to eliminate the problem behavior

1. Teach him the skills by illustrating it to him. If you have a rubber doll, spread some peanut butter on the butt area and use tissue paper to wipe it neatly. Let him do it himself, and if he gets it right, reward him immediately. You can do this exercise in the toilet to aid in better understanding.

2. Praticalise it with him. So, the next time he is done pooping, instead of wiping his butt, give him some tissue to do it himself. It helps if you bring the doll and repeat the action to him while holding out his reward.

3. Be patient. I hope you know he won't learn it the very first day, but the good thing is that we are one step closer to a good result.

4. Decide to remove all the current reinforcement. You will have to stop going into the toilet with them at some point, but you must be attentive to prevent or manage accidents.

If they mess up the bathroom or don't clean properly, refrain from giving them any attention at the moment. You can help them clean up, but nothing more.

5. Make sure your child is okay with the texture of the issue. I worked with parents who were complaining about their daughter's terrible toilet skills.

The mother was already stretched and decided to continue wiping her butt and cleaning the toilet since her daughter refused to learn. After my observation, I found out that the child didn't like tissue and would prefer wipes.

6. Explore a Bidet option if your child's sensitivity won't let him learn how to use the toilet tissue.

However, don't give up teaching them to use tissue since a wipe or bigot is not standard in other restrooms, to avoid your child having good toilet skills only at home.

How to Combine Positive Reinforcement and Extinction to Achieve behavioral change.

Using extinction as a behavior modification technique involves withholding reinforcement for an unwanted behavior, while positive reinforcement entails rewarding a child for a positive behavior. When practiced together, these two strategies decrease the problem behavior while increasing the desired behavior over time.

Imagine your child takes off his clothes outside often; here's how you could use extinction and positive reinforcement to make sure he always stays dressed:

Identify the Behavior: Clearly define the behavior you want to target. In this case, it's your child taking off their clothes outside.

Remove Reinforcement: Determine what may be reinforcing the behavior. For instance, taking off clothes outside might lead to attention from you, a sense of freedom, sensory input, or other types of reinforcement.

Avoid providing any form of attention or support when the behavior occurs. This means no verbal reprimands, laughter, or different responses that might inadvertently reinforce the behavior.

Consistency: It's crucial to be consistent in your approach. Ensure everyone involved in your child's care is on the same page with you and follows the same plan.

Provide Alternative Behaviors: Teach your child an alternative that is appropriate. For instance, you could encourage your child to express their desire for sensory input or freedom in alternative ways, such as telling you they don't wear a particular cloth when they are dressing instead of taking it off outside.

Positive Reinforcement for Appropriate Behavior: Reinforce alternative behaviors you'd like to see instead of removing clothes. When your child engages in appropriate behaviors, provide positive reinforcement, such as praise, rewards, or access to preferred activities.

Time and Patience: Extinction can take time, and the behavior might initially increase before decreasing (known as an extinction burst). Be patient and consistent in your approach.

Supervision and Safety: While implementing extinction, it's essential to prioritize safety. Ensure your child's environment is safe and closely supervise them to prevent any potential harm.

Remember, using extinction can be challenging, and it's essential to consult with a qualified behavior specialist or therapist who can provide guidance tailored to your child's specific needs. They can help you create a comprehensive behavior plan and provide ongoing support to ensure the best possible outcomes.

TAKE HOME

1. Although the period of extinction burst is worrisome and frustrating, you should not stop implementing this strategy except on one condition--that they harm themselves or others around them.

2. Most autistic children develop problems behaviors because they use them to get access to something, they want but can't communicate properly.

3. It is important to always identify why your child engages in a problem behavior as it helps you decide how to correct it.

CHAPTER SIX
DIFFERENTIAL REINFORCEMENT

"Even for parents of children that are not on the spectrum, there is no such thing as a normal child." - Violet Stevens.

Differential reinforcement is another technique to teach your autistic child good behaviors and weaken the problematic ones. Differential reinforcement follows the line of thought that since a child developed a problem behavior because it is functional to them,

If you want to weaken that behavior, all you need to do is stop reinforcing the problem behavior while simultaneously introducing a reinforcement to strengthen a different behavior.

In other words, differential reinforcement refers to reinforcing a target behavior (positive) while removing reinforcement from a target behavior (negative). Here's a practical example: Imagine your child always takes his clothes off.

You can use differential reinforcement to make him to stay dressed by rewarding him every hour he completes without taking off his clothes.

At the end of this chapter, you will be able to know when to use this training method and the specific type of differential reinforcement to leverage and also understand how to pair it with other methods to teach your child new skills and improve existing skills.

Differential reinforcement has five types:

- Differential Reinforcement of Alternate behavior (DRA)
- Differential Reinforcement of Incompatible behavior (DRI)
- Differential reinforcement of other behavior
- Differential Reinforcement of low rates (DRL)
- Differential Reinforcement of high rates (DRH)

DRA is employed when there is a predetermined target behavior alternative to the problem behavior. Let's use the door-banging child again to exemplify this type of reinforcement. So, you will ignore the child banging the door but open the door for the child if they look at you and point to the door or ask you to help them open the door.

DRI is a behavioral modification technique that involves strengthening a behavior incompatible with the problem behavior, thereby weakening the display of the problem behavior.

For example, if your child has a problem behavior of hitting to express his frustration, you can correct it by reinforcing the use of words to express their emotions.

Speaking (the positive behavior) and hitting (the negative behavior) are incompatible, meaning that the learner cannot exhibit both of them simultaneously.

The success of this type of differential reinforcement is dependent on identifying an inconsistent behavior with the problem behavior and consistently reinforcing it.

DRO refers to reinforcing the absence of a specific unwanted behavior during a predetermined period. This method differs from the two above in that it focuses on the lack of the unwanted behavior and does not necessarily reinforce another behavior as an alternative.

For example, if your child frequently hits his head on the wall (problem behavior). A reinforcer is introduced to strengthen the absence of that negative behavior in a predetermined time.

Let's say, after five minutes of not hitting their head on the wall, they are rewarded. The timer resets if the child hits their head on the wall before the stipulated time.

What this differential reinforcement does is that, it helps you gradually decrease the occurrence of unwanted behavior by rewarding periods of non-engagement in that behavior.

DRL is concerned with reducing a problem behavior by reinforcing instances of behavior that occur at a lower rate than the initial occurrence of the unwanted behavior.

This method is employed when the goal of the behavioral change is not the elimination of the behavior but moderation.

For example, suppose an autistic child flaps her hand excessively. In that case, her parents may decide to reduce the hand flapping and not necessarily eliminate it because it does not cause her pain.

To implement this strategy, you have to identify the current frequency of the habit and set a reduction goal. Suppose the child flaps her hand 30-35 times every 10 minutes.

You can set a goal to reduce it to 15-20 every ten minutes; whenever this goal is reached, the child is rewarded. Over time, you can revise the reinforcement criterion to reduce the frequency further.

DRH is the opposite of DHL. The main objective of this strategy is to increase the desired behavior's frequency. With this kind of differential reinforcement, desired behaviors are reinforced with the sole aim of increasing its frequency.

For example, if a desired behavior is 'greeting' and the child greets only her mom and class teacher, you can set a goal to increase greeting from just those two people to other people around. As the learner continues, the criterion for reinforcement can be gradually increased.

HOW TO USE DIFFERENTIAL REINFORCEMENT

Here is the step-by-step procedure to use differential reinforcement to teach your child desirable behaviors and discontinue undesirable ones:

1. Identify the problem behavior you need to change. The question is, what behavior is unwanted? What attitude needs to be corrected?

2. Determine the type of differential reinforcement most suitable for your child to learn the desired behavior or unlearn the undesired one. We have described five types of differential reinforcement, and you have to choose one.

3. Identify the specific behavior you are reinforcing. To use differential reinforcement, the problem behavior is just one part; you need to know the alternative behavior you want to strengthen.

4. Choose a reinforcement. Your choice should be personalized to your child. Remember that a reinforcer is what your child loves and willing to work for.

5. Create the opportunity for them to practice their skills. It would help if you looked for opportunities to allow them to practice the new skill. You can also set up situations to ensure the craft is practiced and reinforced rather than wait till any chance comes naturally.

6. Reinforce the skill when noticed. After a desired skill is practiced, reinforce that skill immediately using one of your chosen reinforcers.

7. Always make sure to evaluate the process and keep accurate documentation. Keeping a record of this process helps you give accounts to the professionals you may be working with and enables you to understand your child's journey.

DIFFERENTIAL REINFORCEMENT: How to achieve a behavioral change in your child (Biting)

It's common knowledge that biting is an aggressive act. Suppose you notice that your child engages in biting himself or others, you need to help them stop it. Differential reinforcement can help you achieve that behavioral change.

First, you need to understand the function of biting for your child or why they are engaging in biting. The two main reasons why your child may be exhibiting aggressive behavior like biting are sensory challenges and communication.

Sensory challenges

Autism and sensory issues are closely related, as it is well recognized. It might be challenging for children with autism to meet their sensory needs. Your youngster may start biting if they have problems satisfying oral sensory needs. When this desire is not satisfied, frustration can result in what appears to be violent behavior toward others.

Communication

Biting can be a way of communication for your child. According to the Autism Treatment Centre, if your child can achieve what they want from you faster by biting you than speaking to you, they may choose to bite more frequently. They could also bite out of anger at being unable to express themselves.

HOW TO STOP YOUR CHILD WITH AUTISM FROM BITING

Identify why they bite. Your child is biting for a reason and if they accomplish their goal with biting, they may never stop biting. If your child is chewing out of boredom or biting out of frustration, it helps to keep them on a predictable schedule.

Select the strategy to use to stop them from biting. After identifying why they bite, choose a procedure to help them change their behavior.

Let's go with INCOMPATIBLE differential reinforcement. This strategy can prevent your child from biting someone because they will use their mouth to do an incompatible behavior with biting.

Give your child another alternative behavior to engage in with their mouth that is incompatible with biting and reward them as they do it. The following behaviors are not compatible with biting: having a snack, blowing bubbles, chewing gum (if your child can chew gum safely)

In conclusion, differential reinforcement helps you change your child's undesirable behavior by reinforcing an alternative behavior, strengthening an incompatible behavior, reducing problem behavior, or encouraging other behaviors except the negative one.

This learning strategy has helped many people to achieve applaudable growth with their children, and you, too, can implement it to achieve the desired result.

TAKE HOME

1. If you want to weaken an undesirable behavior, you must stop reinforcing it while simultaneously introducing a reinforcement to strengthen a different behavior.

2. Keep a comprehensive journal, as it will help you make a data-based decision on what to continue and discontinue after talking to your medical support during your journey.

3. You can adopt the DRL to reduce a problem behavior if the behavior is not harmful. For example, most stimming does not cause harm but needs to be reduced.

CHAPTER SEVEN

EMOTIONAL REGULATION

"Autism is not a puzzle to be solved, but a journey to be embarked upon with love and understanding."

Emotions are the reactions that we feel in response to different situations. In other words, different circumstances trigger different emotions. For example; if you lost your phone or something valuable to you, you may feel sad or angry.

Furthermore, emotions have three main characteristics and they include subjective experience, physiological response and behavioral response.

The subjective experience refers to the fact that no two people experience the exact emotions because we are different. If you and I received bad news, the emotion I will feel will differ from yours.

And even if we both feel sad, it is to different degrees. Again, the subjectivity of emotion is also pictured in the sense that the emotion you experience may be a blend of more than one emotion.

The physiological response of our emotion covers the physiological reactions that occur with emotions. These actions are involuntary body responses. For example, when you are facing a dangerous situation, your body is prepared automatically to face challenges.

The behavioral response refers to the expression of emotions. It is from the behavioral responses of people that we are able to decipher their emotions.

Identifying and interpreting the emotions of people around us enables communication effectively. Every one of us experience emotions and it makes us who we are. And it has a strong influence on your daily life decisions.

However, when we are unable to control our emotions especially the big emotions, we hurt ourselves and people around us. Your child may not naturally have the ability to control their emotions but you can teach them how to do so.

Emotional regulation refers to the process by which individuals influence which emotions they have, when they have them, and how they experience and express their feelings.

Emotional regulation can be automatic or controlled, conscious or unconscious, and may have effects at one or more points in the emotion producing process." Emotional regulation involves the following:

Initiating actions triggered by emotions, inhibiting actions triggered by emotions, modulating responses triggered by emotions.

Benefits of emotions

1. Emotions are motivational. Some kind of emotion encourage you to take action to reach a specific goal. For example; imagine you have an examination and have not studied. The fear of failing that exam can motivate you to read your books.

2. Emotions help you stay out of trouble. Emotions equips the body to take action. For example, if you see a wild animal in a jungle, the fear you feel triggers the bodies to fight or flight response that helps you escape the danger.

3. Emotion influences your choices. Your mental state per time about a specific circumstance influences your decision. So, if you feel sad about a negative situation, you make a decision to avoid getting into scenarios that will bring you sadness again.

4. Emotion enhances your relationship with others. When people understand how your child's feels, they will be able to build a better relationship with them and vice versa.

5. Emotion helps your child understand other people. When a child is able to identify and interpret the emotions of people around them accurately, that child is able to build deeper and meaningful relationship.

Why is emotional regulation important?

1. Academic performance: When your child is able to control their emotions, they are able to focus on their academics.

Most autistic children that are sent out of school were not sent home because of learning disabilities but because they find it difficult to control their emotion.

If your child experiences a hot temper that he harms his classmates, the school will not want him in the school premises.

2. Functional life skills: Emotional regulation is a life skill that every individual needs to function independently. Teaching your child emotional regulation will help him control his emotions.

3. Social interactions: No man is an island of his own. Hence, conversations must take place. Emotion regulation will help your child relate with their peers and even adults. When people always get depressed and push others away, it may lead to people always staying away from them.

4. Emotional regulation enhances verbal and non-verbal communication to take place.

How To Teach Your Autistic Child Emotional Regulation

The objective of teaching your child emotional regulation is not to turn them into 'normal' children or make sure they stop embarrassing you with their meltdowns. Rather, you are helping your child to learn to identify, interpret and control their emotions.

Teaching an autistic child how to regulate emotions is characterized into different stages and they include:

1. **Recognising Emotions.**

This involves making your child aware of the emotions they feel. Your child feels frustrated because they don't even know how they feel and can't control themselves. They allow the feelings to control them and they devise all the weird ways possible to cope.

Let me give you a vivid example; imagine that you won a prize and you scream, you are experiencing happiness and joy. In the same way, when your child expresses such emotions, often times she is not aware that she is happy or that happiness emotion was triggered by good news. So, it is your responsibility to let them know.

The next question on your mind is; why do I help them recognize their feeling beyond telling them? Below I have shown you six practical ways to help them identify what emotions they are feeling:

I. Labeling: This refers to naming emotions that are expressed around you. As people around you expresses emotions, make sure to tell your child the name of that emotion and the indicator. For example; you are watching the television with your child and her favorite character is smiling, you could say; "Hey! Look Tommy is smiling, that means he's happy"

II. Describe their emotions: When your child expresses an emotion, you can point out the emotion by describing it. It helps them recognize it the next time they express such emotion. For example, if they have a sweaty palm and you know they are nervous about something; "you have a sweaty palm and you are breathing fast. You must be afraid."

III. Point out your emotional responses. You can identify your emotional responses as you discuss with your kids. For example; "I am so happy. Thumbs up"

IV. Help your child express what they feel. Like we discussed, the physiological responses of the emotions are felt. When your child is expressing an emotion, help they work out how their body feels. "You look angry. Is your head banging?"

V. Show them a picture of emotion responses. If you have pictures of sweaty palms, faster heartbeat, this exercise helps them to know the common indicator of a particular feeling and is able to link their emotions to the identified emotion when they experience that indicator.

VI. Draw feeling Exercise. Asking your child to draw how they feel is a good way to allow your child express what they feel. You can have a predesigned pictures with the names of emotions. So, when the child is happy, they draw the shape of the happy picture.

VII. Engage in emotion activity with your child. The emotion activity game means that you name a particular emotion and act it out. For example; "Happy" is the selected emotion. You or your child will go ahead and demonstrate the gestures of a happy person. You can also act the action and let your child guess what emotion you have demonstrated.

VIII. Practice emotional skills through play. During play, your child has the opportunity to express emotions like happiness and other emotions. This practice prepares them to express their feelings better when playing with other children.

Understanding Emotions

The moment your child is able to identify their emotion, you need to help them understand what each emotion means and why they are feeling that way, it helps them accept their feelings. You help your children to understand their feeling by talking about it.

1. Tell them that it is normal to experience emotions. Your child depending on how old they are having to hear you tell them that they are fine for feeling happy, sad, angry. They should know that everyone has emotions.

2. Explain to them how emotions happen. They need to understand that their thoughts can influence their emotions. If they think that you will scold them for what they did or did not do, they may become afraid.

Common Mistakes Parents Make During Their Child's Meltdown

Often times, parents make some bad choices in an attempt to help their child during meltdowns. Although these mistakes are often done ignorantly, they come with consequences these children live with. To avoid this reality for your child, desist from the following Meltdown mistakes parent make.

1. Cancel every form of punishment: Meltdowns are not tantrums so punishing your child is punishing a child for being helpless.

A couple narrated to me how a professional encouraged them to force their children to stay in school and reduce meltdowns by introducing punishment.

If you currently do this, please stop it. It will only lead to your child having terrible traumas. No amount of punishment will stop your child from experiencing meltdown.

2. Talking to them: Some parents think by telling their child to calm down or sit down, they control their child but that's not true.

Your children may respond better to pictures at that time. Rather than talk to them, remind them their coping strategies using pictures.

3. Grabbing them: You know that autistic children have sensory aversions and being touched during meltdown maybe one of them. You should only touch them when they are in danger or hurting someone else.

Managing Emotions

Managing emotion means controlling the extremes of your emotions. Your child will experience big emotions from time to time and it is important that they are able to manage their emotions. But they can't do it without your help.

I. Relaxation exercises: Many times, the outburst of emotions of your kids could be averted by engaging in relaxation exercises.

II. Sensory Stimulation: This involves satisfying your child's sensory needs.

III. Break time: This refers to allowing your kid take a break from a task or an activity to help them manage their emotions.

IV. Change of activity: Sometimes we you notice that your child is getting tired agitated or bored with an activity, you can switch to another one to prevent him or her from experiencing one of those big emotions.

V. Physical Activity: Variety of physical activities can help your child manage his emotions. Just find the one that works best for you.

How To Manage a Meltdown

I. Identify Triggers and eliminate them. This is the first step to managing meltdown. Some parents have told me how they reduced the frequency of their children's meltdown by identifying and removing their triggers from their environment.

The triggers are things that propels your child to have a meltdown. It could be anything. Your responsibility is to keep observing them and identifying them.

II. Spot the routine and intervene. Often, before your child has a meltdown, you can see the signs. In situations like this, you should distort the process.

For example; your baby is already getting stressed in a particular environment. If you get the cue early enough and take them to a different environment where they prefer to stay. In addition, some children get to their meltdown through a routine. If you interrupt the routine wisely, you may prevent the meltdown.

III. Refuse to be embarrassed. I am not even going to lie, managing a child's meltdown in public can be frustrating. One day when my son was experiencing a meltdown years ago, some clueless woman whispered loud enough for me to hear that I was a psychopathic mother.

I remember being livid but at the end of the day, I have come to realized that my top priority is my child and never the passerby.

IV. Think Safety. Depending on your child's meltdown manifestation, make sure they're not hurting themselves or anyone around. If you notice that the environment is not conducive, consider taking them to a better place.

V. Ask your child how you can help: It is important to ask your child what they think you can do to make them feel better. Some children can answer this question during the meltdown while MOST children can only have this conversation after the meltdown is gone.

VI. Ask For Help: Like I will always say, you are not alone and don't ever think you are, you can ask for help from a professional or autism community you are a member of or other parents of autistic children you have bonded with.

Remember that your child is unique so copying a successful meltdown strategy of someone else may not work all the time.

VII. Check in with your family: Let everyone that cares understand what's going on. You may not always be present and even if you are, they are family and they deserve to be aware. Their being aware will help them understand your child better.

TAKE HOME

1. Emotional regulation refers to the process by which individuals influence which emotions they have, when they have them, and how they experience and express their feelings.

2. The easiest way of reducing the frequency of your children's meltdown is by identifying and removing their triggers from their environment.

3. The process of emotional regulation for autistic child includes emotion identification, emotional understand of emotion and emotion management.

CHAPTER EIGHT
SOCIAL SKILLS DEVELOPMENT

"God created autism to help offset the excessive number of boring people on earth" - Unknown.

Social skills refer to the skills a child has to enhance their daily communication with their environment. Social skills include verbal and nonverbal. Building your social skills can improve every area of your child's life.

The lack of social competence is one of the most challenging things autistic children experiences. A child is said to be competent in social skills when they have the combination of cognitive, social interaction, social communication, social and emotional, and social and behavioral skills.

Why you should teach your child social skills:

1. Good social skills helps your child to build healthy relationships: Your child will need connections to grow and thrive, and they can only make one if they have basic communication skills.

2. It increases their academic performance: Your child will perform better if they have good communication skills.

3. Avoid loneliness: Your child should be able to interact with people around you or be at risk of loneliness, which can lead to another negative outcome like depression.

4. It encourages social acceptance: We all want a sense of belonging, and social skills are essential to make it happen.

5. To build healthy self-esteem, your child must know how to express their thoughts and opinions to people around them.

Examples of social skills

Sharing: This refers to the willingness of a child to give a part of their things to others. It could be a cookie or even their toys. A child who is good at sharing things will make and maintain friends.

Children are likely to start sharing their stuff with people around them from age two. An excellent way to ensure your child learns to share is to praise or reward them for sharing and not necessarily forcing them to share.

Cooperation: Your child has cooperation skills when working with others to achieve a common goal. Kids like this respect requests from other kids and contribute to the task they want to achieve.

This skill helps a child to fit into a social community. Typically, children start cooperating effectively from three years. To help your child become more cooperative, create opportunities where the whole family works together to achieve a particular purpose.

Listening: This is a core communication skill which another skill stem from. And I hope you know that listening is not merely keeping quiet but understanding what someone else is saying.

With listening, your child can do well at school and even in different aspects of his life. The best way to help your child develop good listening skills is to provide them the opportunity to listen. For example, you can read to your children and ask them questions to ensure they are listening to you.

Following directions: This skill entails your child carrying out a task as you have directed. This skill is essential because your child will learn to do things immediately and avoid negative consequences. You have a role to play in your child developing this skill because you give the direction. If you provide an ambiguous instruction, they may miss it.

Making eye contact: Making eye contact is one of the common social skills that children develop, but some children struggle to make eye contact. It makes sense to know why it is difficult for them to make eye contact and help them develop the skill gradually.

Use Manners: Every child gets to learn basic manners from the people around them. When your child doesn't say please or thank you, when necessary, you must encourage them to do so. The best way to help your child cultivate good manners is to be a role model.

Milestones for Children's Development

Always pay attention to some common social skills child development milestone especially as a first-time mother or father.

For example, if you know that a baby of 0-2 months should be following moving objects with their eyes, begin making cooing sounds, and smiling in response to familiar people, but your four months old child has not started doing any of it, you will definitely start asking questions.

Other common social skill development milestone include;

- 2-4 months, are most likely to start babbling and making other vowel sounds.

- 4-6 months, makes consonant sounds, responds to "no", begins to wave bye-bye.

- At 6-9 months, the baby begins to say first words, such as "mama" and "dada", understands simple commands, such as "give me", plays peek-a-boo.

- And at 9-12 months, they start saying other 2-3 words other than "mama" and "dada". They begin to understand simple questions, such as "Where is the ball?". Also, they imitate simple actions, such as clapping hands.

This is just a general overview of infant development milestones. Every child develops at their own pace, but it is just a guideline to what to except and know what you need to start teaching your child.

How to Help an autistic child to develop social skills.

As you already know, your child is wired differently and has challenges developing some social skills. However, some strategies will help them grow and improve the social skills that they need, and we will discuss some of them.

Practice Play: Some adults assume that playing is a way for children to scatter the whole space and would prefer them to sit quietly on the couch with their eyes fixed on the television or sleep. Play is beyond a time when children make noise and mess up the house; it is also when children learn.

As a matter of fact, play is one of the best mediums to teach your child some social skills. So, I want you to intentionally play with your child regularly to teach them social skills such as turn-taking, coping with winning and losing, following directions, and so on.

There are different plays you can do with your child. You can use toys to do pretend play. This may involve you feeding the teddy or putting the teddy to sleep and allowing your child to do the same. Other game ideas are card games, hide and seek, etc.

While playing any game with your child, have a goal in mind and structure the game to attain that goal. For example, if you want to teach your child how to follow the rules, you could play card games and make sure to establish the rules for them from the onset.

Then, make sure to correct him whenever they miss it. Another beautiful thing about teaching your kids social skills with play is that you can focus on one skill using different sports, which will help them learn that particular skill and use it in different situations.

Encourage them with praise: If you appreciate the progress your child is making, be vocal to encourage them to do more. This strategy is applicable when you see your child practicing a social skill like making eye contact that they rarely do.

Children of any age are likely to respond positively to praise. When you praise your child, you are nurturing their confidence. Henceforth, praise your child when they exhibit a desirable attitude. For example, "Bob, allowing your friend to play with your toy is nice. Give me a high five."

Use Social Stories: As the name suggests, social stories are crafted to depict a social situation for autistic children and help them learn how to behave in such cases. The idea behind this strategy is that autistic children see the world differently and misunderstand some social cues, such as body language, or to show someone is angry with eye contact.

Moreover, these stories will help them act accordingly by establishing details about the social situation, the events in the case, and how the child in the story is expected to act. So, the child can pick cues they usually won't notice and respond rightly. Social stories are written from the child's perspective.

Social skills Training: There are many formal social skill training you can leverage. Make sure to understand the concept of the one you will use. The best way to choose is to ask for recommendations from fellow parents.

Visual supports: Visual support refers to every optical technique you use to encourage your child to learn a new social skill or practice a previously discovered skill. For example, if they are talking to you but are not making eye contact, you can use a picture to remind them that they should do that. Examples of visual supports include pictures, words, prompt cards, and more.

Collaborate with teachers: You don't have to only practice these social skills at home; discuss them with your child's teachers so that they monitor them in school too. I have seen many children who only use skills they learn in one environment and can't use them in the other environment.

How to Measure Your Child's Social Skills

Beyond teaching your children social skills, you must also assess their social competence. Social competence is a context-dependent construct; thus, an instrument suitable to one context may not be ideal for another.

There are many ways of evaluating if your strategies are working. I will discuss eight instruments according to the International Conference of

Teaching and Learning: Language, Literature, and Linguistics.

1. Moving toward functional Social Competence Autism Social Skills Checklist. This instrument was designed by Hanzlick et al., 2010. This checklist aimed to discover the social competence of children aged three to twenty-two years.

The Educator is expected to rate the child's performance in the following areas: joint attention, Greeting, Play/Leisure skills, Self-regulation, conversation, perspective-taking, social problem-solving/critical thinking skills, Friendship, and Life skills.

2. The Autism Social Skills Profile (ASSP) is designed to measure the social functioning dimension of an autistic child. The Educator and the child's teachers are expected to rate the child in the following aspects:

Social reciprocity, social participation or avoidance, and detrimental social behavior. This instrument is suitable for children from six to seventeen years.

3. Triad Social Skills (Stone et al., 2010) measures three essential aspects of the social competence of a child, which include social skills, social behavior, and Child interaction.

This is prepared for a six to twelve-year-old child, and the rating is done differently by the child, the Educator, and the parents.

4. The Social Skills Checklist (University of Washington, 2004) is used to measure your child's social skills, such as social play and emotional development, emotional regulation, and group skills. The rating process is carried out by your child's educator.

5. Social Skills Improvement System Rating Scales (Gresham et al., 2011) is an instrument used to measure the social competency of a three to eighteen-year-old child.

The significant areas measured are social skills, problem behaviors, and Academic Competence. The social skills include communication, cooperation, assertion, responsibility, empathy, engagement, and self-control.

The measured Problem behaviors include externalizing, bullying, hyperactivity/inattention, internalizing, and Autism Spectrum. Academic competence provides reading, math, and motivation to learn.

6. Social Responsiveness Scale (Bruni 2014): This evaluation instrument measures the social awareness, social cognition, social communication, social motivation, restricted interests, and repetitive behavior of eighteen-year-old children.

7. The Devereaux Student Strengths Assessment (LeBuffe, Shapiro & Naglieri, 2009) is an evaluation instrument to measure the social-emotional competence of a three to fourteen years child in areas such as self-awareness, social awareness, self-management, goal-directed behavior, relationship skills, personal responsibility, decision making, and optimistic thinking.

In conclusion, your autistic child can be competent in social communication if you teach them the social skills. Find out the functional social skills they lack and teach them. Remember that you have to teach them in the way that they would understand. Also, evaluate the skills from time to time to know your progress.

TAKE HOME

1. Play is one of the best mediums to teach your child some skills

2. Your child will need connections to grow and thrive, and they can only make one if they have basic communication skills.

3. Building your social skills can improve every area of your child's life.

CHAPTER NINE
SENSORY REGULATION

"The most interesting people you will meet are the ones that don't fit into your average cardboard box. They will make their own boxes," - Dr. Temple Gradin.

Mary (not her real name) was diagnosed of autism at twenty-two. She was in college at that time. She had series of meltdowns. These meltdowns never came when she was at home.

Apparently, her dad was also autistic and have the same sensory issues with her. She never had troubles with her sensory demands at home because, it had been customized to suit her dad, so she just coped well but going to the college environment, everything changed.

What does this mean for you? It means that if you identify the sensory needs of your child and satisfy them, they will live more independent lives.

Having unique sensitivities to certain types of sensory input can be problematic in our daily lives because every setting especially in the public domain cannot be customized to fit your sensory needs.

Imagine a child who is hypersensitivity to bright colors, she is not always guaranteed to have her a unique classroom because other children who love to learn with bright color illustration maybe sharing the class with her.

A number of children with autism employ stimming to help them with their sensory seeking so as to keep their sensory systems in balance. Example of such stimming include repetitive movements, sounds, or fidgeting.

If you notice any stimming habit, don't be quick to plan to eliminate them because they can help your child stay calm or relieve stress.

Sensory Challenges

Children with autism display certain sensory challenges and they include:

A. Sensory overload: Children with autism may be easily overwhelmed by sensory input, such as noise, light, touch, taste, smell, or movement. This can cause them to feel anxious, stressed, or even have a meltdown. For example; Covering ears or eyes, chewing on non-food items regularly etc.

B. Sensory seeking: Some children with autism may crave sensory input and engage in repetitive behaviors, such as hand flapping or rocking, in order to get it. This can be a way for them to self-regulate and calm down.

Some children manifest sensory seeking in the following ways; continuous mobility such as jumping, spinning or crashing into things, high rate of stimming, such as hand flapping, making repetitive noises or rocking back and forth, making loud noise or not talking at all, hardly noticing that they are hungry, in pain or want to use the rest room.

C. Sensory defensiveness: Other children with autism may be sensitive to certain sensory input and avoid it at all costs. This can include things like loud noises, bright lights, certain textures, or certain smells.

Not every child with autism will experience sensory challenges in the same way. Some children may only be sensitive to certain types of sensory input, while others may be overwhelmed by all types of sensory input. Another thing to note is that sensory challenges can change over time. A child who is sensory seeking at one age may become sensory defensive at another age.

Sensory Regulation Strategies

There are several ways to teach your kids to accommodate their sensory issues such as customizing the environment to suit their sensory needs, leveraging tools that satisfy their sensory needs, developing new habits. In a few situations, children can adopt different sensory accommodation for different setting. Below are sensory regulations you should try out:

1. Identify your child's sensory triggers. When you understand the sensory issues of your child, it will help you teach them how to accommodate them.

So, you will have to know what sights, sounds, smells, tastes, textures, or movements make your child feel overwhelmed or uncomfortable? Start to avoid identified triggers or develop strategies to cope with them.

Create a sensory-friendly environment. This could involve reducing noise levels, using soft lighting, providing comfortable seating, and limiting visual distractions.

You can also create a sensory room; where the child can go to relax and stim. Furthermore, your child can get a sensory-friendly classroom. As a parent to an autistic child, you have the right to request for reasonable sensory accommodations at their school.

Consider discussing your child's sensory accommodations at their school with their Individualized Educational Program (IEP) team or consider a 504 plan.

IEP is a document that spells special education instruction, supports, and services kids need to make progress and thrive in school. 504 plan refers to the plan that supports disabled children attending an elementary or secondary educational institution by giving them access to conducive environment to ensure academic success.

3. Teach the child self-regulation strategies. This could involve deep breathing, relaxation techniques, or fidget toys. You can also help the child develop a sensory diet of activities that help them feel calm and regulated.

Examples of accommodations for hypersensitivity: using light covers, sunglasses or a hat under fluorescent lights, wearing ear plugs or headphones in noisy environments, working in spaces with a closed door or high walls, avoiding strongly scented products, adjusting schedules to avoid crowds etc.

Examples of accommodations for hyposensitivity: visual supports for those who have difficulty processing spoken information, using fidget toys, chewies and other sensory tools, arranging furniture to provide safe, open spaces, eating foods with strong flavors or mixed textures, weighted blankets, lap pads or clothing that provides deep pressure and more

4. Be patient and understanding. Sensory regulation can be challenging for autistic children, so it's important to be patient and understanding. Always make your child know that it's okay for them to feel overwhelmed and that you're there to help.

3. Get help from professionals. If you're struggling to help your child with sensory regulation, talk to your therapist. They can provide additional support and resources.

TAKE HOME

1. As a parent to an autistic child, you have the right to request for reasonable sensory accommodations at their school.

2. When you understand the sensory issues of your child, it will teach you how to accommodate them.

3. A number of children with autism employ stimming to help them with their sensory seeking so as to keep their sensory systems in balance.

CHAPTER TEN
EXPLORE THERAPY

"I am an autism parent. We have good days, bad days and days we try to forget."

Several therapies can help your child improve his or her abilities and simultaneously reduce symptoms. These therapies produce better results when introduced early.

The American Academy of Pediatrics (AAP) recommends you start researching therapy immediately you suspect your child is autistic and not wait until a formal diagnosis that takes time.

In this chapter, we will examine the few therapies you can explore. Make sure to select the therapy that caters for your child's unique needs at the moment.

Remember you don't have to make that decision alone as you can get recommendation from experts or experienced parents.

Speech Therapy

Speech therapy for autistic children focuses on improving communication skills and addressing language challenges. It employs various techniques to enhance speech, language comprehension, social interaction, and nonverbal communication.

Therapists work to tailor interventions to each child's unique needs, helping them develop effective communication abilities and fostering better interaction with others.

Why Should I consider speech therapy for my autistic child?

Speech therapy can provide numerous benefits for autistic children and some of them are as follows:

Improved Communication Skills: Speech therapy can help autistic children develop their language skills, including speech sounds, vocabulary, grammar, and understanding of language, enabling them to better express themselves and interact with others.

Enhanced Social Interaction: Developing communication abilities through speech therapy can aid in fostering better social interactions. As communication improves, your child may find it easier to engage in conversations, make friends, and navigate social situations.

Reduced Frustration: Communication challenges can lead to frustration and behavioral issues. Speech therapy can help minimize this frustration by providing effective communication tools, reducing the likelihood of meltdowns or tantrums.

Increased Independence: As your child becomes more proficient in communication, they may gain greater independence in daily activities, such as expressing their needs, making choices, and participating in routines.

It's important to collaborate with a qualified speech-language pathologist to create a customized therapy plan tailored to your child's unique needs and strengths.

Autistic children might struggle with maintaining focus during therapy sessions, making it difficult to engage in activities and follow instructions. To overcome this issue, break sessions into shorter, more manageable segments.

Use activities that align with your child's interests to maintain their attention. Visual schedules, timers, and sensory breaks can also help manage attention spans.

Autistic children can have sensory sensitivities that make certain therapy activities overwhelming or uncomfortable. However, you can gradually introduce sensory stimuli and adapt therapy environments to accommodate sensitivities.

Work with the therapist to identify sensory-friendly strategies and tools that can create a more comfortable and effective learning environment. For instance, if **your child is sensitive to touch, use alternative ways to practice speech, such as using communication apps or drawing pictures that convey their thoughts**.

Some autistic children struggle with verbal communication, making it challenging to express their thoughts and participate in therapy activities. In such situation, it is good to incorporate alternative communication methods, such as augmentative and alternative communication (AAC) systems.

These could include picture exchange systems, communication apps, or sign language. The therapist can help choose the best method based on your child's abilities.

Children who are resistant to change may not cooperate with therapy. For example: Your child might resist trying new communication techniques or engaging in therapy activities due to their preference for routines.

A helpful tip is to introduce changes and new activities bit by bit. For instance, if your child enjoys a particular game, the therapist could modify it to incorporate speech exercises. This helps the child become more comfortable with change over time.

NOTE:

1. Speech therapy aims to improve your child's speech clarity, vocabulary, grammar, and social communication skills. It can help them express themselves more effectively, interact with others, and reduce frustration by providing effective communication tools.

2. The frequency of sessions depends on your child's individual needs and progress. Initially, sessions might be more frequent (e.g., once or twice a week), gradually reducing as your child makes progress. Your speech-language pathologist will recommend a schedule that suits your child's goals.

3. You can reinforce speech therapy at home by practicing communication activities recommended by the speech therapist. Engage in conversations, read books together, play interactive games, and encourage your child to use newly learned communication skills in real-life situations.

4. Speech therapists create individualized therapy plans based on your child's strengths and challenges. They might use visual aids, alternative communication methods, and play-based activities tailored to your child's interests to enhance engagement and progress.

5. Collaborate with the speech therapist to adapt activities to your child's sensory preferences. Gradually introduce sensory stimuli and provide breaks when needed. By finding a balance between sensory-friendly strategies and therapy goals, you can help your child feel more comfortable and engaged.

Occupational therapy (OT)

Occupational therapy (OT) is a type of therapy that helps people of all ages participate in the activities of their daily lives. It can be used to address a variety of challenges, including those related to autism spectrum disorder (ASD).

Occupational therapy for autistic children can help with a range of skills, such as:

Motor skills: Occupational therapy can help your child develop both fine and gross motor skill. Fine skills are the skills needed to use small muscles, such as those in the hands and fingers. OT can help with tasks such as buttoning, zipping, and writing.

Gross motor skills are the skills needed to move the large muscles of the body like such as walking, running, and jumping.

Sensory processing: This is how the body interprets information from the senses, such as touch, taste, smell, sight, and hearing. OT can help children who are oversensitive or under-sensitive to sensory input.

Social skills: These are the skills needed to interact with others. OT can help children with ASD learn how to play, share, and take turns.

Communication skills: These are the skills needed to express oneself and understand others. OT can help children with ASD learn how to use verbal and nonverbal communication.

Occupational therapy can be provided in a variety of settings, such as schools, clinics, and homes. The frequency and duration of the sessions will vary depending on the child's needs.

Challenges Of Occupational Therapy

Here are four challenges encountered during occupational therapy and their possible solutions:

Motivational barriers: You may not be motivated to participate in occupational therapy, either because you do not see the need for it or because they are feeling discouraged.

The therapist can address this challenge by working with you to identify your goals and create a therapy plan that is tailored to their needs and interests. They can also provide positive reinforcement and encouragement throughout the treatment process.

Opportunity barriers: Often, you may not have the opportunity to participate in occupational therapy due to financial constraints, lack of transportation, or other factors.

Some professionals can collaborate with you to find ways to overcome these barriers, such as providing financial assistance, arranging transportation, or finding a therapy location that is convenient for you.

Communication barriers: In some situations, your child may have difficulty communicating with their occupational therapist due to language barriers, cognitive impairments, or other factors.

The therapist can address this challenge by using interpreters, simplifying their language, or using alternative communication methods, such as pictures or gestures.

Environmental barriers: Some people encounter troubles in occupational therapy due to environmental factors, such as a lack of accessibility or safety. This trouble can be addressed by working with the patient's environment, such as modifying their home or workplace, or providing assistive devices.

SOCIAL SKILLS TRAINING

Social skills training is a type of intervention that helps children with autism spectrum disorder (ASD) learn the skills they need to interact with others in a socially appropriate way.

This can include things like learning how to take turns, how to make eye contact, and how to express their emotions in a healthy way.

Social skills training can be done in a variety of settings, including individual therapy, group therapy, and in the classroom. The specific techniques used will vary depending on the child's individual needs and abilities. However, some common techniques include:

Role-playing: This involves acting out different social scenarios so that the child can practice their skills in a safe and controlled environment.

Modeling: This involves the therapist or teacher demonstrating the desired behavior for the child to copy.

Social stories: These are brief stories that teach the child about specific social concepts or skills.

Video modeling: This involves showing the child videos of other children interacting in a socially appropriate way.

Reinforcement: This involves rewarding the child for using the desired skills.

Social skills training can be a very effective intervention for children with ASD.

However, it is important to note that it is not a quick fix. It takes time and practice for children to learn these skills. Additionally, social skills training should be just one part of a comprehensive treatment plan for children with ASD.

Here are some additional things to keep in mind about social skills training for autistic children:

- The earlier the intervention begins, the better.

- The child's parents or caregivers should be involved in the training process.

- The training should be tailored to the child's individual needs and abilities.

- The training should be ongoing and consistent.

- If you are concerned about your child's social skills, talk to their doctor or therapist. They can help you assess your child's needs and develop a treatment plan that is right for them.

Benefits of Social Skills Training for Autistic Children

The major benefits of social skills training for autistic children are as follows:

- Social skills training can help children with ASD learn how to interact with others in a more appropriate and effective way. This can include things like learning how to take turns, how to make eye contact, and how to express their emotions in a healthy way.

- As children with ASD learn and practice social skills, they may start to feel more confident in their ability to interact with others. This can lead to increased self-esteem and a better overall sense of well-being.

- Social skill training plays a role in reducing anxiety and stress: Social interactions can be stressful for children with ASD, especially if they feel like they are not being understood or accepted. Social skills training can help children learn how to manage their anxiety and stress in social situations.

- Social skills are important for academic success. Children who are able to interact with others in a positive way are more likely to be successful in school. In addition to these benefits, social skills training can also help children with ASD develop a better understanding of themselves and others. It can also help them learn how to cope with challenges and build positive relationships.

Challenges of Social Skill Training

Unfortunately, social skill training can be hindered by the following drawbacks:

- Children with autism may not be motivated to participate in social skills training because they do not see the need for it or because they are feeling discouraged. One way to address this challenge is to make the training as fun and engaging as possible. You can also try to connect the training to something that your child is interested in, such as playing games or making friends.

- Children with autism may have difficulty understanding the social concepts and skills that are being taught in training. The use of visual aids and concrete examples may help them understand better. You can also break down the concepts into smaller steps.

- Children with autism may have difficulty applying the social skills they learn in training to real-world situations. Hence, providing opportunities for your child to practice the skills in a safe and controlled environment is an excellent idea. You can also provide feedback and reinforcement when the child uses the skills correctly.

- Children with autism may have difficulty generalizing the social skills they learn to new situations. One way to address this challenge is to gradually expose the child to different situations and gradually increase the difficulty of the situations. You can also provide the child with strategies for coping with challenging situations.

Physical Therapy (PT)

Physical therapy (PT) is a health care profession that helps people of all ages improve their movement and function. PT can be beneficial for autistic children who may have challenges with their: gross motor skills, fine motor skills, sensory processing, balance and coordination, self-care skills, and social skills

PT can be done individually or in a group setting. It can be used to address specific challenges or as part of a comprehensive treatment plan. The specific interventions used will vary depending on your child's individual needs and goals.

Physical Therapy Interventions

Some common PT interventions for autistic children include:

i. **Proprioceptive input:** This involves providing deep pressure to the body, which can help to improve balance, coordination, and sensory processing.

ii. **Visual tracking:** This involves following moving objects with the eyes, which can help to improve eye-hand coordination and attention.

iii. **Motor planning:** This involves teaching children how to plan and execute movements, which can help to improve gross and fine motor skills.

iv. **Social skills training:** This involves teaching children how to interact with others in a positive and appropriate way, which can help to improve social skills.

v. **Therapy balls:** These are large, inflatable balls that can be used to help children improve their balance and coordination.

vi. **Weighted vests:** These vests can be used to provide deep pressure to the body, which can help to improve balance, coordination, and sensory processing.

vii. **Stretching exercises:** These exercises can help to improve flexibility and range of motion.

Viii. **Strength training exercises:** These exercises can help to improve muscle strength and endurance.

ix. **Functional activities:** These activities are designed to help children improve their ability to perform everyday tasks, such as getting dressed, eating, and using the bathroom.

PT can be a beneficial intervention for autistic children. It can help to improve their physical, social, and emotional well-being.

If you are concerned about your child's development, talk to their doctor or therapist. They can help you assess your child's needs and develop a treatment plan that is right for them.

Cognitive-behavioral therapy (CBT)

Cognitive-behavioral therapy (CBT) is a type of psychotherapy that helps people change the way they think, feel, and behave. It is based on the idea that our thoughts, feelings, and behaviors are all interconnected, and that by changing one of these things, we can change the others.

CBT has been shown to be effective in treating a variety of mental health conditions, including autism spectrum disorder (ASD). In CBT for ASD, the therapist works with the child to identify and challenge negative thoughts and beliefs that are contributing to their difficulties. The therapist also teaches the child coping skills to help them manage their emotions and behaviors.

One of the most common CBT techniques used for children with ASD is social skills training. This involves teaching the child how to interact with others in a more appropriate and effective way. Social skills training can include teaching the child how to make eye contact, how to take turns talking, and how to read social cues.

Another CBT technique that is often used for children with ASD is cognitive restructuring. This involves helping the child to identify and challenge negative thoughts and beliefs.

For example, a child with ASD might think "I'm always going to be alone" or "I'm not good enough." The therapist would help the child to challenge these thoughts by providing evidence to the contrary.

CBT can be an effective treatment for children with ASD, but it is important to find a therapist who is experienced in working with this population.

CBT can be delivered in individual or group settings, and the frequency of sessions will vary depending on the child's needs. Here are some of the benefits of CBT for autistic children:

- It leads to social and communication skills improvement.

- It enhances emotions and behaviors management.

- It can help children to develop coping skills for dealing with stress and anxiety.

- It can help your child to improve their self-esteem and confidence.

If you are considering CBT for your child with ASD, it is important to talk to the professional you are working with. They can help you to decide if CBT is right for your child and can recommend a therapist who is experienced in working with this population.

Play therapy

Play therapy is a type of psychotherapy that uses play to help children express their thoughts, feelings, and experiences. It is based on the idea that children communicate through play, and that by understanding their play, we can better understand their needs.

Play therapy can be used to help children with a variety of mental health conditions, including autism spectrum disorder (ASD).

In play therapy for ASD, the therapist creates a safe and accepting environment where the child can feel free to explore their thoughts and feelings through play. The therapist may use toys, games, and other creative materials to help the child communicate.

In play therapy, the therapist aims to improve the child's social skills. This can be done by helping the child learn how to interact with others, how to take turns, and how to resolve conflicts.

Play therapy can also help children to develop their communication skills, their problem-solving skills, and their self-esteem.

Play therapy is a flexible and adaptable therapy that can be tailored to the individual needs of the child. It is a non-threatening and non-judgmental approach that can be very effective in helping children with ASD.

Some benefits of play therapy for your autistic child are as follows:

- It can help your child to express their thoughts and feelings in a safe and non-threatening way.

- It enhances the development of your child social and communication skills.

- It help them to learn how to cope with stress and anxiety.

- It can help your child to develop their self-esteem and confidence.

- It can help your child to make progress in other areas of their lives, such as school and relationships.

Sensory Integration Therapy (SIT)

Sensory integration therapy (SIT) is a type of therapy that helps children with autism spectrum disorder (ASD) process and make sense of sensory information. Children with ASD often have difficulty with sensory processing, which can lead to problems with attention, behavior, and learning.

SIT is based on the idea that the brain needs to integrate sensory information in order to function properly.

When the brain is not able to integrate sensory information effectively, it can lead to problems with sensory processing.

SIT can help children with ASD to improve their sensory processing by providing them with opportunities to experience different sensory inputs in a safe and controlled environment. The therapist will use a variety of activities and materials to help the child learn how to attend to and make sense of sensory information.

Some of the activities that may be used in SIT include:

1. Deep pressure activities, such as weighted vests or blankets

2. Proprioceptive activities, such as balancing or jumping

3. Vestibular activities, such as swinging or spinning

4. Tactile activities, such as brushing or squeezing

5. Visual activities, such as looking at different textures or colors

6. Auditory activities, such as listening to different sounds

SIT can be an effective therapy for children with ASD, but it is important to find a therapist who is experienced in working with this population. SIT can be delivered in individual or group settings, and the frequency of sessions will vary depending on the child's needs.

Benefits of SIT

Some of the benefits of SIT include:

- It can help your child to improve their attention and focus.

- It is useful when trying to teach your child to regulate their emotions.

- It improves your child's motor skills.

- It can help your child to improve their social skills.

- It can help your child to reduce their anxiety and stress.

Music therapy and Art therapy

Music therapy and art therapy are both forms of creative arts therapies that can be used to help children with autism spectrum disorder (ASD).

These therapies use the creative process to help children express themselves, communicate, and learn.

While music therapy is the use of music to improve a person's physical, emotional, cognitive, and social well-being. Art therapy is the use of art materials and techniques to help people express themselves and explore their emotions.

These therapies can be used to help children with ASD in a variety of ways, such as: improving communication skills, reducing anxiety and stress, increasing self-esteem, developing social skills, improving motor skills, promoting relaxation.

Both music therapy and art therapy can be effective treatments for children with ASD. The best approach for your child will depend on their individual needs and preferences.

Benefits of Music therapy and art therapy for your child

- Children are encouraged to express themselves in a safe and non-threatening way.
- It propels children to communicate their thoughts and feelings.
- They can help your child to relax and reduce stress.
- These therapy leads to social skills development.
- They can help your child to improve their self-esteem.
- They can help your child to learn new skills.

TAKE HOME

1. Therapists work to tailor interventions to each child's unique needs.

2. Music and art therapies use the creative process to help children express themselves, communicate, and learn.

3. Speech therapy aims to improve your child's speech clarity, vocabulary, grammar, and social communication skills. It can help them express themselves more effectively, interact with others, and reduce frustration by providing effective communication tools.

Therapy will go a long way to help your child. Your responsibility is to select the best therapy for your child and work with a good professional to achieve the best result.

CHAPTER ELEVEN

LET'S HELP YOU FIND YOUR THERAPIST

"When people pursue their interest, especially those that are on the autism spectrum, they have a better chance at succeeding in life"

Autism can make it difficult for children to communicate and interact with others. A therapist can help your child learn how to communicate more effectively and develop social skills.

Also, a therapist can help you understand your child's behavior and develop strategies for managing it so that they can reach their full potential.

But choosing an autism specialist can be a daunting task, and the objective of this chapter is to help you figure it out.

I have listed ten things you should consider when choosing a professional to work with. Following these tips below will increase your chances of finding a qualified and experienced specialist who can help your child reach their full potential.

1. **The specialist's qualifications and experience:** Make sure the specialist is qualified to work with children with autism. They may have a degree in a relevant field, such as psychology, speech-language pathology, or occupational therapy but must have experience working with children with autism.

2. **The specialist's approach to therapy:** Find out the kind of therapy the specialist uses. Some specialists use behavioral therapy, while others use play therapy or art therapy.

There is no one right approach, so find one that you think will be a good fit for your child.

3. **The specialist's communication style:** Make sure you feel comfortable communicating with the specialist. They should be able to explain the therapy process to you in a way that you understand. They should also be able to answer your questions.

4. **The specialist's availability:** Ask about the professional's availability to work with your child. You may need to find someone who is available during the times that work best for your family.

5. **The specialist's fees:** Inquire about the specialist's charges for their services. Make sure you can afford the fees before you make a decision.

6. **The specialist's location:** Ask about where the specialist is located. You may need to find someone who is close to your home or school.

7. **The specialist's willingness to collaborate with other professionals:** Your child may also be seeing other professionals, such as a doctor or a teacher. Make sure the specialist is willing to collaborate with these professionals to create a comprehensive treatment plan for your child.

8. **The specialist's willingness to work with you as a parent:** You are your child's most important advocate. Make sure the specialist is willing to work with you to create a treatment plan that meets your child's individual needs.

9. **The specialist's willingness to be flexible:** Things don't always go according to plan. Make sure the specialist is willing to be flexible and adjust the treatment plan as needed.

10. **Your gut feeling**: Ultimately, you need to feel comfortable with the specialist you choose. If you have a good feeling about someone, then that's a good sign.

Autism Formal Diagnosis Process

Not every autistic child gets the chance to undergo a formal diagnosis process but it is important as you may need it in working with your therapist or even to access insurance and the following is the process it takes:

Screening: The first step is to screen your child for autism. This can be done by your pediatrician or another healthcare provider.

There are a number of different screening tools available, but some of the most common include the Modified Checklist for Autism in Toddlers, Revised with Follow-Up (M-CHAT-R/F) and the Autism Spectrum Screening Questionnaire (ASSQ).

Evaluation: If your child screens positive for autism, they will need to be evaluated by a specialist.

This could be a developmental pediatrician, a psychologist, or a team of professionals. The evaluation will typically include a number of different tests and assessments, such as:

i. Observations of your child's behavior

ii. Interviews with you and other caregivers

iii. Standardized tests of development and language

Iv. Medical tests to rule out other conditions

Diagnosis: The specialist will use the results of the evaluation to make a diagnosis of autism. There is no single test that can definitively diagnose autism, so the diagnosis is based on a combination of factors.

The autism diagnosis process can be long and complex, but it is important to get your child evaluated if you are concerned about their development.

Early diagnosis and intervention can make a big difference in the lives of children with autism.

The time it takes to get an autism diagnosis in the United States, United Kingdom, and other states can vary depending on a number of factors, such as the availability of services in your area and the severity of your child's symptoms. In general, the process can take anywhere from a few months to a year or more.

What Is the Cost of Autism Diagnosis?

The estimated cost of autism diagnosis in the United States can vary depending on a number of factors, including the type of assessment, the location, and the provider. However, it is typically in the range of $3,000 to $15,000.

Here are some of the factors that can affect the cost of autism diagnosis:

The type of assessment: There are a variety of different autism assessments available, and the cost will vary depending on the type of assessment. Some common types of assessments include:

Developmental and behavioral assessments: These assessments assess a child's development and behavior in a variety of areas, such as communication, social skills, and play.

Medical assessments: These assessments may include genetic testing, and imaging tests.

Neuropsychological assessments: These assessments assess a child's cognitive abilities, such as attention, memory, and problem-solving.

The location: The cost of autism diagnosis can vary depending on the location. In general, it is more expensive to have an autism assessment in a major city than in a rural area.

The provider: The cost of autism diagnosis can also vary depending on the provider. Some providers charge more than others.

There are a number of resources available to help families pay for autism diagnosis and treatment. Some of these resources include:

Medicaid: Medicaid is a government health insurance program that provides coverage for low-income individuals and families. Some states cover autism diagnosis and treatment under Medicaid.

CHIP: CHIP is a government health insurance program for children. Some states cover autism diagnosis and treatment under CHIP.

Private insurance: Some private insurance plans cover autism diagnosis and treatment. However, coverage can vary depending on the plan.

Charities: There are a number of charitable organization that provide financial assistance for autism diagnosis and treatment.

What Is the Scope of Your Health Insurance Coverage?

The scope of health insurance coverage for children with autism in the United States can vary depending on the specific insurance plan. However, some common benefits that may be covered include:

- Autism diagnosis and evaluation: Most insurance plans will cover the cost of an autism diagnosis and evaluation, which can be expensive.

- ABA therapy: Applied behavior analysis (ABA) therapy is a type of therapy that is often used to treat autism. ABA therapy can be expensive, but many insurance plans will cover it.

- Speech therapy: Speech therapy can help children with autism improve their communication skills. Speech therapy is often covered by insurance, but the coverage may vary depending on the plan.

- Occupational therapy: Occupational therapy can help children with autism develop their fine motor skills and learn how to cope with sensory challenges. Occupational therapy is often covered by insurance, but the coverage may vary depending on the plan.

- Physical therapy: Physical therapy can help children with autism improve their gross motor skills and coordination. Physical therapy is often covered by insurance, but the coverage may vary depending on the plan.

- Medication: Some children with autism may need medication to manage their symptoms. Insurance plans vary in terms of whether they cover medication for autism.

- Support groups and respite care: Support groups and respite care can provide families of children with autism with much-needed support. Some insurance plans will cover the cost of support groups and respite care, but the coverage may vary depending on the plan.

It is important to check with your specific insurance plan to see what benefits are covered for children with autism. You can also contact your state's autism insurance clearinghouse for more information.

In addition to insurance, there are a number of other resources available to help families pay for autism treatment. Some of these resources include:

- The Autism Speaks National Resource Center: The Autism Speaks National Resource Center can help families find information and resources about autism, including insurance coverage.

- The National Autism Association: The National Autism Association can help families find financial assistance for autism treatment.

- The Autism Insurance Tracker: The Autism Insurance Tracker is a website that provides information about autism insurance coverage in different states.

TAKE HOME

1. A therapist can help your child learn how to communicate more effectively and develop social skills.

2. Medicaid is a government health insurance program that provides coverage for low-income individuals and families.

Every child is a gift to the world. Your role as a parent is to give them the support, they need to improve their social interaction, emotional regulation, sensory regulation.

You can help them learn new skills and unlearn undesirable habits through positive reinforcement, extinction, differential reinforcement and more. There is no one way of achieving your goal as all children are unique. That's why you must work with a professional and seek recommendation from more experienced parents

Authors Note

Dear Reader,

I hope you enjoyed reading my book as much as I enjoyed writing it. Your feedback means the world to me, and I'd be incredibly grateful if you could take a moment to *leave a review.*

Reviews not only brighten an author's day but also help other potential readers discover the book.

So, Please, share your thoughts, insights and feelings about this book. Thank you for your support.

Warmest wishes,

Sharon Daven

References

Anon (2022). Raising Children Network. *Recognising, understanding and managing emotions: autistic children and teenagers*

https://raisingchildren.net.au/autism/development/social-emotional-development/recognising-understanding-emotions-autistic-children-teens

Anon (2017) Raising Children Network. *Social skills for children with autism spectrum disorder*

https://raisingchildren.net.au/autism/communicating-relationships/connecting/social-skills-for-children-with-asd

Anon. American Speech-Language-Hearing Association. *Autism spectrum disorder: overview*

http://www.asha.org/practice-portal/clinical-topics/autism/

Carrie. C (2015) Speech and language Kids. *5 Principles of Speech Therapy for Children with Autism* https://www.speechandlanguagekids.com/5-principles-of-speech-therapy-autism/

Emma H. (2022) www.youtube.com 7 Early Signs of Autism Every Parent Should Know https://youtu.be/WRRF4NZB3WQ?si=pqASMmX2VI1noz_H

Heather J. N., Giacomo V., Cheryl D., (2013) Cognition & Emotion. *Are emotion impairments unique to, universal, or specific in autism spectrum disorder? A comprehensive review* 27(6) 1042-1061 DOI: 10.1080/02699931.2012.762900

Jane E. H, Jennifer S. C., (2014) Emotion *Back to basics: A naturalistic assessment of the experience and regulation of emotion.* 14(5) 878-891 DOI: 10.1037/a0037231

James H. (2022) www.youtube.com. *Heidi Mavir - Your Child Is Not Broken - Autism, ADHD, and what to do when school isn't working By* https://youtu.be/RrgjFlQzorU?si=BbHpacwOeLlURao1

Roseann C. S., Teal B., Zoe M., Patricia F., Joanne H., Elke V. H., Regina F., Benjamin L. Jocelyn S., Donna K. (2013) Journal of Autism and Developmental Disorders. An *Intervention for sensory difficulties in children with autism: A Randomized Trial*. 44 (7) DOI: 10.1007/s10803-013-1983-8
https://www.ncbi.nlm.nih.gov/pmc/articles/PMC4057638/

Madhuleena R. C. (2019) Positive Psychology What is emotion regulation? + 6 emotional skills and strategies https://positivepsychology.com/emotion-regulation/

Mirko U., Antonia H. (2013) Journal of Autism and Developmental Disorders. *Recognition of emotions in autism: A formal meta-analysis* 43 (7) 1517-1526 DOI: 10.1007/s10803-012-1695-5

Nikolaus K., Matthias F. L., Ulrich W. E., Jana K., Anne D., Mathias B., Christian S., Martin B. (2011) Journal of Personality Disorders *Dissociation predicts poor response to dialectial behavioral therapy in female patients with borderline personality* disorder 25(4) 432-447 DOI: 10.1521/pedi.2011.25.4.432

Printed in Great Britain
by Amazon